TRENCH TALK/
TRENCH LIFE

TRENCH TALK/ TRENCH LIFE

A BEGINNER'S GUIDE TO WORLD WAR ONE

FREDRIC WINKOWSKI

FOREWORD / DR. STEPHEN BULL

Glitterati
INCORPORATED

New York | London

In memory of my brother, James Winkowski

First published in 2017 by

Glitterati
INCORPORATED
New York | London

New York Office: 630 Ninth Ave, Ste 603, New York, NY 10036
Telephone: 212 362 9119

London Office: 1 Rona Road, London NW3 2HY
Tel/Fax +44 (0) 207 267 9739

www.GlitteratiIncorporated.com
media@GlitteratiIncorporated.com for inquiries

First edition, 2017
Library of Congress Cataloging-in-Publication data is available from the publisher.

Hardcover edition
ISBN: 978-1-943876-46-4
Printed and bound in China
10 9 8 7 6 5 4 3 2 1

Contents

"FOR WITH THE DIGGING OF THE TRENCHES A SELF-CONTAINED WORLD WITH ITS OWN INTERNAL LOGICS AND REGIMES WAS BORN, AND A SOLDIER WHO DID NOT UNDERSTAND AND ADHERE TO THE MOST IMPORTANT OF THESE WAS AT SERIOUS DISADVANTAGE."

FOREWORD

GETTING CLOSER

DR. STEPHEN BULL

We all have a picture of the Western Front in our mind's eye. Almost certainly this involves trenches, machine gun fire, shell bursts, mud, suffering, death and vermin. Yet what we see in France and Belgium today counter-points such images to an almost absurd degree: a sanitised landscape that almost makes it hard to believe the war ever happened. The tangible remains are, for the most part, well-kept cemeteries and grand memorials. Farmland appears serene and untouched until suddenly a shell is unearthed. Far too often landscapes are poorly explained by clichés and the broad brush pictures painted by the popular media.

Getting genuinely closer to life in the trenches and the often illusive detail of the scene is very much harder. For this there are several good reasons. The lapse of a century, the advance of technology and the changing attitudes of the times should be obvious, but there are other more subtle factors to take into account. One, all too often overlooked, is that the war and the people fighting it changed markedly over the period 1914-1918. For at the start the "Great War," what became "World War I" to Americans, was a war of movement. Its manoeuvres and uniforms, and the parts played by cavalry infantry and artillery were based on late nineteenth century norms. In many quarters the war was joined with real enthusiasm and in the hopeful expectation it would soon be over. The long war, the appearance of "Trench warfare," and a basically static front, were initially viewed as aberrations, even with incomprehension. The way that the war was fought and the way in which people thought and spoke about it changed swiftly and dramatically.

For with the digging of the trenches a self-contained world with its own internal logics and regimes was born, and a soldier who did not understand and adhere to the most important of these was at serious disadvantage. Failure to recognise dangers like parts of a line covered by snipers, how to move without attracting attention, or how to get warm without showing light or smoke might prove fatal. In an often claustrophobic atmosphere of dugouts and trenches, in which living enemies were seldom seen and heads not shown over parapets before dark, men devised new language to describe both the things around them and the various hardships and predicaments they faced. On all sides new ways of speaking were tinged with humour and cynicism, and littered with shortcuts or allusions making it difficult for the uninitiated to follow what was going on,

"ON ALL SIDES
NEW WAYS OF
SPEAKING WERE
TINGED WITH HUMOUR
AND CYNICISM,
AND LITTERED WITH
SHORTCUTS OR
ALLUSIONS."

even during the war itself. A distance was created between the front line fighting soldier and the rear areas, a gulf between the trenches and civilian life at home. Sometimes the fighting soldier seemed to have more in common with his enemy across "No Man's Land" than he did with those he left behind. Even after the war a gap of understanding remained between those who had been there, and those who had not.

What Fredric Winkowski does here is shine a light on the experience of the front by looking at things through the eye and the patois of the soldiers themselves. Knowing what they said puts us one small step closer to knowing what they thought and felt.

9

"ONE STATEMENT
SO DISRUPTED MY
NORMALLY PLACID VIEW
OF THE WORLD, THAT
IN RETROSPECT, IT IS
CLEARLY THE ORIGIN
OF THIS BOOK."

PREFACE

Historical insight rarely comes to a third-grader, but it did so on a November the eleventh, many decades ago. One statement so disrupted my normally placid view of the world, that in retrospect, it is clearly the origin of this book.

It seemed unusual, at least to me, that Miss Golden, my unsmiling third-grade teacher, had taught my much older brothers years before. But long before that, she had also taught my mother, back in the immeasurably ancient year of 1919. And because my mother often talked about her school days, I felt a connection to her early life, and my imagined scenes from those years had an almost tangible reality for me. It was as if I might someday happen upon a hidden staircase, in an empty house, that could lead back to 1919.

During the school year, on November 11, on the day that was then called Armistice Day, Miss Golden made a statement that was literally burned into my consciousness. Despite the class's excitement with veteran's red paper poppies being distributed, Miss Golden said this was a sad day, a day of remembrance. It was the day, Miss Golden said, in 1918 the Armistice had been signed and the war ended. And on that day, after the signing, and when peace had at last come to the Western Front, her brother had been killed. There it was, the circle was unbroken, and there I was in 1918, stunned and trying to understand what it meant.

And over the years, to this day, this is a question that has fascinated and at times obsessed me. What was the "what" and "why" of that war, now one hundred years distant? The voice of that remote lady still whispers a sad tale. What happened? And I am again in 1918 and this book is my hidden staircase backward through time. And at last I have discovered information about those men who were killed on 11/11/1918.

Some years following that, I became, among other things (such as the class artist), an occasional junior-high school antiquarian. And it was WWI that fascinated me most. The dark and smelly Plaza Book Store in downtown Albany, New York, was endlessly enchanting. Among the clutter, and aroma of garlic, there were great treasures. *Over the Top*, by Arthur Guy Empey, a 1918 compendium of all things related to life in trenches, cost twenty-five cents, and was priceless. It is in fact a major influence for this current book.

Later as a professional art director and illustrator I tended toward projects that dealt either with history, or the world of the future. My first book was *The Martian Crystal Egg* and in it I created a WWI-era vision of Mars. Later still I had the incredible good fortune to meet others in my field who also had a fixation on the "War to End All Wars." For a book of my airplane photography, I was graciously allowed to fly with a formation of Fokker triplanes along the coast of Maine.

But most impressive to me, I was able to get behind the scenes, and examine impressive collections of uniforms, photographs, weapons, and the mundane paraphernalia of trench life. Two of those great collectors and historians were Ed Vebell and Rick Keller. Without their generous help this book truly would not be possible. Ed had been an illustrator for *Stars and Stripes*, the army newspaper in WWII, and he did the marvelous drawings of the Nazi prisoners during the Nuremberg trials. Ed was a terrific photographer, and took pictures of many small arms from Rick's collection, and I played the relatively minor role of photo assistant. And it was through Ed and Rick's connections that I was able to participate and photograph at a WWI reenactment event, accurately dressed in a German tunic and steel helmet. The event was living history; however, in just a few hours, I was "killed" five times, including by a rifle grenade, poison gas, and a French automatic rifle team. I was surprised by the historical accuracy at the event, and very impressed that it was presented as a dignified tribute to the "fallen" of the Great War. Just to complete the record, I've also published perhaps ten photographic books dealing with the history of transportation, and they featured substantial coverage of the WWI era.

I have long felt the reading public, both adult and young adult, needed a concise, richly illustrated, and evocative book on World War I. This is an era easily trivialized, or even lost down the memory hole of history. The WWI Centennial offered an opportunity to create a fresh approach to the subject. It seemed to me a "browser's book" in the format of a guidebook could be both an introduction to the subject, and a permanent reference work. And since even today, historians disagree about many aspects of the war, I went back to many original sources, and featured the troop's own "trench vernacular." This like all slang is a language apart, created to give voice to a unique experience.

As an illustrator and art director, to me the visual aspect of any project has to be equal to the text. There are many excellent photographs from WWI, yet somehow they never really work together in book form. Number one, the quality is inconsistent, which is understandable given the demanding conditions under which the photographs were created. Number two is that many of the photographs are clearly propaganda shots, created for publications or some governmental agency. They just look phony. Number three is that photographs never properly illustrate the text. The intent of the original photographer was probably to make snapshots of friends, or perhaps show a panorama of some sort. It is unlikely he would be interested in what, to him, were the mundane elements of everyday life. Plus, it was not the photographic style of the time to photograph close-up shots. The answer is illustration. It can do now what photography forgot to do then. But clearly reference photographs are vital for accurate drawings. My illustration process has two steps: first a quick tracing from reference material, and then creating the intricate interior line-work that gives the drawing form and character. The effect is that of an engraving, which is also appropriate for the time period. For those with copyright concerns, just about all drawings were done from photographs published before 1927, and are no longer covered by copyright. Another point to make is that I love drawing people and things from this time period, and so doing the drawings was a pleasure.

And to say it once again, working on this book has been my hidden staircase back to 1919, and a connection with my own history.

"THE LANGUAGE IS NOT
SO IMMEDIATELY EVIDENT,
BUT IN A WAY MORE
INTENSELY PERSONAL TO
THEIR CIRCUMSTANCES,
STRUGGLES, AND EVENTS."

INTRODUCTION

In 1914 Germany was the wunderkind of Europe. It saw itself as the world leader in science and culture. But it felt surrounded by dangerous, hostile nations, primarily France, which wanted revenge after losing the Franco-Prussian War in 1871. Many Germans also felt anger toward Britain because they believed British wealth was undeserved, extracted from its colonies that spanned the globe, although Germany wanted also to expand and desired similar colonies.

The war that erupted was really about defending the French. The Germans were sure they could win over France and England and the United States came to their defense. France, Britain, and Russia had treaties of mutual defense, and were known as the Triple Entente. Germany, the Austro-Hungarian Empire, and Turkey were known as the Central Powers, and they had a similar alliance. These are potentially unstable alliances that could cause a war if the unexpected happened, which it did with the assassination of an Austro-Hungarian nobleman. There were demands and threats between Austria and Russia; treaties were invoked, and within weeks all the nations of Europe were at war with waving flags and much excitement.

The German Kaiser's armies invaded neutral Belgium, attempting to outflank French forces. Belgium's defenses were overwhelmed, alleged German war crimes incensed the world, and Germany next pressed on into France.

The French army also reeled backward, seemingly defeated. However, with exhaüsted enemy forces only eighteen miles from Paris, France struck back in the Battle of the Marne and the German advance was halted. The casualties, especially for France, were huge and soon both sides dug in and did not move: The trench line extended from the North Sea to Switzerland.

Vast battles were fought, especially with the French at Verdun and the British at the Somme. Millions of people were lost, but the Germans were well entrenched at the Hindenburg line and all attempts to dislodge them were both costly and futile.

The situation finally changed with the end of the Russian Revolution, when Germany's armies from the Eastern Front were released to become became available for the great Spring Offensive of 1918. Allied defenses were obliterated and victory for Germany appeared almost certain. But history repeats itself at the Second Battle of the Marne: With all German reserves gone and America and the Allies at last vigorously attacking the enemy, the war suddenly ended at 11 am on November 11, 1918.

As the form of warfare fought from the trenches of World War I had its own style of life, so did the "slang" language that developed in those trenches by which the three allied soldier groups communicated within their own groups—the *Poilu*, the French Army

Soldier; Tommy, the British Army Soldier; and the Doughboy, the American Army Soldier. The chapters of this book follow each of these groups in their trenches and through their languages, appearing in the order in which they entered the war as allies, each lifestyle and language distinctly developed by the brave soldiers who lived their lives and fought their enemies from the trenches—a form of warfare that was not ever used again after the end of World War I, except during the Iran-Iraq conflict from 1980 to 1988.

The unique way these men lived in the trenches will immediately become clear in looking through the pages that follow—showing their armaments, their clothing styles, and their demeanors—in these alien "homes" that were created out of necessity. But the language is something else; not so immediately evident, but in a way more intensely personal to their circumstances, struggles, and events. These three individual designations for naming the allies are actually slang and have no official sanction, yet elicit tremendous evocative power. Just the names themselves may conjure at least a few visions of muddy trenches, with waves of khaki-clad men advancing through a hopelessly lethal battlefield. And there are thousands of additional words in slang words used by the troops of every nation, each with similar evocative power.

Experts on language-theory propose that slang is a legitimate sub-language that evolves inevitably under certain conditions. The main requirement is a group of people, separate from everyone else, often under stress, who need to talk about the events of their daily life when ordinary words don't do the job. Example groups might be cowboys, or criminals, or even the old time hobo. In all cases just the simple use of slang creates a sense of group identity, the classic "us against them."

Looking briefly at hobo slang might be useful since it was inventive and witty, it was from the same era as WORLD WAR ONE, and shared some words with the doughboy's lexicon. A reader knowing nothing about hobos, upon seeing an evocative list of hobo words is immediately swept into the hobo jungles. An "accommodation" is a local freight train, "balling the jack" is traveling at high speed, to "yank" is to be arrested, "egg" is a criminal, and "gone with the birds" is to grab a ride south for the winter. Hobo words had a kind of poetry, although used and derived from the bottom of lower class speech, so were dismissed as unacceptable as common parlance. The hobo words shared with the doughboy's lingo had a longer life. Examples are, "crums" for lice," axle grease" for butter, "banjo" for a short-handle shovel, "teapot" for locomotive, and "slum" for a kind of stew. Of course WORLD WAR ONE soldier's idiom focused on the war. Because eighty-percent of all casualties were caused by the big guns, there were countless names for types of shells—shells both coming and going— and names for guns, the most famous of which was "wizz-bang," a relatively small but lethal German artillery piece. And there were many euphemisms for death: "gone west" being the most common. Death was so commonplace in the trenches that speaking the actual word was considered distasteful or unlucky. The situation was something like the nicknames for the "Prince of Darkness," where calling him by his real name was too risky, so "Old Nick," "Scratch," or "Old Harry" were good substitutes.

The question remains as to why we should devote time to thinking about World War One. Isn't it ancient history, maybe less relevant to modern life, even, than study of the Greeks or Romans? One answer is that history, for wont of a better word, is entertaining. Dig into any historic era, and the reader is sure to be rewarded by fascinating stories of every type. However World War One really is unique. It was the first full-blown example of the Machine Age gone awry. It was the original steam-punk war, containing every tool of destruction that technology could devise, and factories could mass-produce. World War One was the hinge of history; whether obvious or not, it changed everything after it, including

five European rulers who had to hang up their crowns. And to some extent it empowered the common man and woman. The social contract between ruler and ruled had to be renegotiated, however imperfectly, as did the social contract between man and woman or husband and wife. With the end of the war the businessman replaced the aristocrat as the rightful arbiter of power; skirts were shorter; literature was less florid; and slang began to get at least a little respect.

There are so many good books devoted to the political and strategic aspects of World War One and this book can add little to those discussions. However, this book is about the millions of peaceful, conservative, honorable men—just ordinary civilians—who marched into impossible situations of foul trenches and the occasional ruinous "Big Shows," or battles. This book is definitely not a history of politics, or battles, or great generals. It is the story of adaptation; and how ordinary men, who liked to think that "their number wasn't up," tried to survive in an extraordinary situation.

"SLANG IS THE
LANGUAGE THAT TAKES
OFF ITS COAT...AND
GETS TO WORK."

—CARL SANDBURG

CHAPTER ONE

TRENCH VERNACULAR

WORDS OF WAR

SAY "OVER THE TOP," "DUD" OR
"CHUM," OR EVEN "WRISTWATCH,"
AND IN A SENSE, YOU'RE ON
YOUR WAY TO THE TRENCHES OF
WORLD WAR I. THESE WORDS, AND
HUNDREDS MORE, ARE EXAMPLES
OF THE PRIVATE LANGUAGE
THAT DEVELOPED ON THE
WESTERN FRONT.

A LIFE IN THE TRENCHES

Poet Carl Sandburg said, "Slang is the language that takes off its coat...and gets to work."

Trench talk is a variety of slang that does exactly that. All these trench words and phrases shown here simply represent a better way to understand that time. It must be remembered that the real heart of this story is the heroism and tenacity displayed by the men who occupied the trenches. They lived and died under conditions that were brutal and unforgiving. And yet these hard-pressed men persevered until the end.

One thing that British troops didn't like about the nickname "Tommy" was that it was so popular with enemy troops. When German and British trench lines were close together, Germans would shout taunts and jeers, derisively calling to "Tommy" with a German accent.

The Original Trench

Sometime in the future, trench warfare may be forgotten, but **trench coats** will probably still be around. It is a classic design, from the era that created other classics, like the light bulb and bicycle. The official army greatcoat was heavy, but the trench coat was light, flexible, waterproof, and for officers only. The two main producers were Burberry and Aquascutum, and each had its own process to create waterproof fabric. Stylish as well as practical, officers could go to their favorite Bond Street tailor, to purchase the style they fancied.

Many words and phrases from WWI have survived, none more indelible than "**over the top**." It paints the essential picture of the Western Front: the rush up the trench ladder, over the sandbag parapet, and into a field of death. Wave after wave of men entered no-man's-land only to be swept away by enemy artillery and machine gun fire. This was Tommy's ultimate moment, alone with his Enfield rifle, his bayonet, his discipline, and his private thoughts.

British Tank Talk

H. G. Wells imagined a kind of tank in 1903 and called it the land iron-clad. When actually proposed to the British military by Winston Churchill in 1915, the name "landship" was used. When finally built, the armored vehicles were code-named "tanks," to disguise their intended use. The first working prototype was called "Mother." Deployed tanks were called "female" tanks when armed with machine guns, and "male" tanks when armed cannons.

TALKING TRENCH

Mad Minute: every morning each British soldier fired his rifle rapidly at the enemy for a minute.

Strafe: the German word for "to worry or confound." Eventually it meant to rake with gunfire, especially from an airplane.

Big Bertha: very large German artillery pieces, usually mounted on flatbed railroad cars.

Storm Troopers: specially trained German troops used to infiltrate enemy lines.

Souvenirs: French for keepsake or memento; entered English language during World War I.

Uncle Sam Nixes "**Sammy**"

What should the American troops in France be called? The name finally settled on was a compromise. Many people liked the name "Sammy," which the troops hated. The army newspaper *Stars and Stripes* declared it unacceptable. "Yankee" offended soldiers from the American South, even though the term "Yank" became a runner-up. The French liked both Sammy and "Amis," which just sounded wrong. But there was the old army term "doughboy." Nobody was quite sure what it meant, but it seemed to fit.

FRANCE
TALKING TRENCH

THE FURY OF MODERN ARTILLERY STOPPED ALL THE WARRING ARMIES IN THEIR TRACKS. LOOKING FOR SOME PROTECTION, THE FRENCH, AS WELL AS THE GERMANS, WERE FORCED TO SEEK SHELTER BELOW THE SURFACE OF THE EARTH. EVENTUALLY A VAST, SEMI-PERMANENT NETWORK OF TRENCHES, BRISTLING WITH ARMED MEN, WOULD DEFINE WARFARE ON THE WESTERN FRONT.

While the concept of a periscope was good, its use could be dangerous, as this quotation illustrates:

> "In passing along the trenches I was offered a periscope, but the moment the end of it appeared above the surface it was saluted by a perfect rain of rifle shots."

The near constant presence of German observation planes meant that most activities, such as routine repairs or troop reinforcements, had to be done at night. During the day, except for a few sentries, the forward-most trench was nearly empty. At night the entire network of trenches was busy with work of all sorts, but still quiet. Clearly it was best not to disturb the German line in any way unless absolutely necessary.

MUSIC

For the WWI French soldier, trench warfare was a brutal and dehumanizing reality. Life in the trenches might be better than participating in an all-out attack, but not always. Fetid water covered the bottoms of trenches and muddy trench walls constantly collapsed. Enemy snipers were an ever-present danger. Just a few yards away no-man's-land was filled with unburied bodies from both armies. At night rats crawled through the trenches looking for any food, especially food stuffed into the sleeping soldiers kit bags. The itching of lice, ticks, and fleas made life seem unbearable. With drinking water scarce, cleanliness was a dream, as unattainable as a furlough to visit home. Even in the quiet sectors, random enemy shells could bring unexpected death. And when things became active, artillery shells of every type screamed overhead. French troops called that *la Musique*.

No man knew who would be next, but those who died had certainly won their *croix de bois* or cross of wood, in the nearby cemetery.

TALKING TRENCH

L'Abri: bunker, dugout, or shelter

Un Boyau: communication trench (literally, intestine) was the entrance to a trench.

Le Créneau: loophole or observation slit in trench for snipers.

Un Moineau: type of Artillery shell; literally, sparrow, because of the sound it made when flying over the soldiers.

Moulin à Café: machine gun; literally, coffee grinder.

La Bouillasse: muck, mud.

P.C.D.F., or "Poor Victims at the Front" (an approximate translation) nickname the exhausted poilus in the trenches gave themselves.

Le Séchoir: barbed wire, or the clothesline. The term referred to soldiers killed and fallen onto the wire, as if hung out to dry.

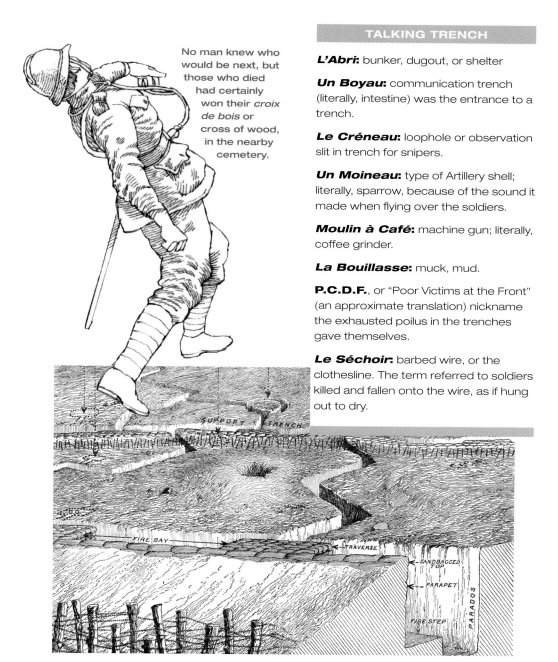

Illustration of trench from the book *First Call* from 1918

23

BRITAIN TALKING TRENCH NO. 1

THE WOUNDED TOMMY WAS ENTITLED TO THE BEST POSSIBLE CARE, BUT IT COULD BE AN UNCERTAIN ROAD BACK HOME.

"I wasn't napoo, but it was a near go. Then I waited for a teakettle, and it was back to Blighty."

TRANSLATION

Napoo or "Napoo-finis" was popular British trench idiom for "all finished up" or "ended." It is based on the French phrase "there is no more" (*il n'y en plus*).

A **near go** is familiar nineteenth-century British slang for "a close call."

The **teakettle** was a steam locomotive, especially a narrow gauge one. The American company Baldwin built the Class 10-12-D shown here. Nearly five hundred were built for service in France with the British. Hospital trains took the wounded to hospitals far behind the lines, or to a port on the English Channel for returning home.

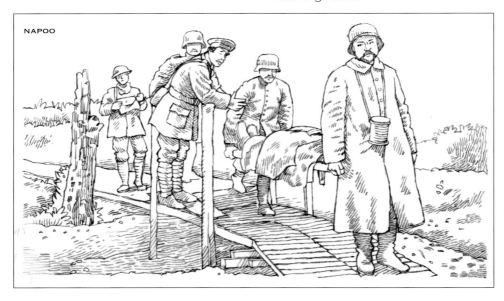

NAPOO

Above: Due to labor shortages, German prisoners of war were required to do useful work of various sorts, such as fixing roads, etc., as well as evacuating British wounded from the battlefield. They did this task with admirable diligence. The cylinder around the German's neck is a gas mask container, since gas attacks might occur at any time.

TEAKETTLE

THE BLIGHTY ONE

Naturally the British soldier in the trenches yearned to return home. Officers could sometime hop a Channel ferry on a weekend, and enjoy theater and dinner in London's West End, and return to the front the following week. Not so for the other ranks. Once a year, or year and a half, they might get a ten-day leave. Essentially, Tommy was in the army for the duration. Was there another way to go home, and stay home? One way was the "Blighty One," **Blighty** being the slang for home. Getting a Blighty One meant being wounded, seriously but not fatally, and not being maimed or debilitated. Such a wound would entail a long, pleasant convalescence back in their Dear Old Blighty.

BRITAIN TALKING TRENCH No. 2

HERE ARE SOME EXAMPLES FROM
THE BRITISH TRENCH LEXICON
THAT CAN BE USED WHEN TALKING
ABOUT THE PREPARATION FOR A
NIGHTTIME TRENCH RAID.

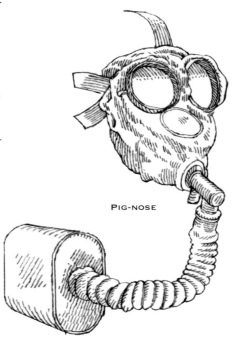

PIG-NOSE

"We wrapped up our putts, took our pig-nose, persuader, and come-alongs, and went out with the Black Hand Gang."

Translation

German troops wore tall, heavy, leather boots. They became even heavier when covered with layers of mud. The British leg wrapping, called **puttees** or **putts**, could be removed, and easily cleaned.

There were several types of gas masks. The British Small Box Respirator (BSBR) with the round snout was called the **pig-nose**. Gas masks were uncomfortable, and not easy to use, and so known as "exasperators."

A night raid on enemy trenches had to be silent, and gunfire was to be avoided. One favorite weapon was a heavy wooden club with protruding nails. The name **persuader** seems well chosen for this one.

PERSUADER

A raid's greatest prize would be to capture and bring back an enemy soldier for interrogation. Once captured, the unfortunate enemy had to keep up with the British raiders as they hurried home. To do this, a **come-along** was used. It was simply a length of barbed wire with a loop that was slipped over the neck, and pulled like a leash.

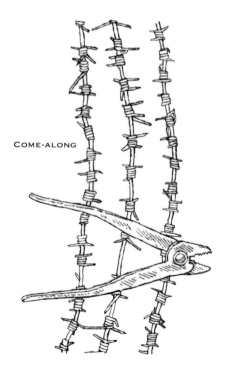

COME-ALONG

NIGHT RAIDS

The boredom of inactive life in the trenches was intolerable to some men, and they would jump at the chance for novelty. A raid on the German trenches was extremely risky, but there was a need for fresh intelligence. And there were always men ready for the job. One such man was the British officer with a German name, Siegfried Sassoon. He was so good at the job, he earned the name **Mad Jack**. Men on these raids ironically called themselves **The Black Hand Gang**, after the fearsome secret society. Sassoon would later become a celebrated anti-war poet and author.

AMERICA TALKING TRENCH

DOUGHBOYS HEADING TO THE WESTERN FRONT WERE WELL ADVISED TO EQUIP THEMSELVES WITH A FEW WORDS AND PHRASES OF BOTH FRENCH AND GERMAN.

Like anyone else, the French could show great hospitality and warmth. One American's memoir describes the family with whom he lived in Soissons.

There was the grandfather who was wary of the Germans, since he had been captured and taken to Germany in the 1871 war. Madame was the perfect mother, sewing on buttons and making delicious meals with meager ingredients. And there were two sons, one entering the army, and one who had been lost on the battlefield, in a common story in France during the war years.

28

NOBON

For young Americans contemplating their trip overseas, the French language seemed quite an obstacle. A 1918 Troy, New York, newspaper printed a list of French place names with phonetic pronunciations:

Humont—Oh-mon
Nasle—Nas-ley
Roulers—Roo-lay
Versailles—Ver-sigh
Yser—Ee-sare

It is easy to see why the British Tommy happily slaughtered the French language throughout the war, calling Roulers "rollers." The doughboy would also approach France's living national treasure with similar casualness.

The author of the wartime book *A Surgeon in Arms* writes:

"The slang of the frontlines resembles a new system of Esperanto, since it takes in, in a cosmopolitan manner, all the languages of the neighborhood, as well as some whose existence may be doubted. For example, '**nobon**' means no good, and is a mixture of English, French, and a disgusted look. "**Napoo**" (which is probably a mutilated form of the French "*il n'y en a plus*—there is no more) has a most versatile meaning, and is used in many different senses. It signifies that some article of the rations is finished, as "the rum is napoo"—a not uncommon state of affairs. At other times it is used as we employ the slang phrase, "nothing doing."

Above: A doughboy helps a boy with grandfather's old bicycle.

Advice for Speaking with French Hosts:

• The French are a polite people, and they expect similar behavior from guests.

• Unlike the reserved British, the French can be temperamental, and they should never be insulted.

• Try not to cringe when being greeted by a man, and kissed on both cheeks.

• Soldiers would sometimes be billeted in French villages near civilians, and the cost of food seemed expensive. Empey advised that despite the high price, doughboys should enjoy French food, since it could often be excellent.

"THE PROUDLY
MUSTACHED,
MUD-SOAKED, AND
UNKEMPT FRENCH
FIGHTING MAN."

CHAPTER TWO

FRANCE WITH THE POILU

POILU

THE POILU WAS THE CITIZEN SOLDIER OF THE FRENCH REPUBLIC. IN CIVILIAN LIFE, MORE OFTEN THAN NOT, HE HAD BEEN A FARMER, AND SO WAS FAMILIAR WITH THE RIGORS OF THE OUTDOOR LIFE. IN TOTAL THERE WERE EIGHT MILLION FRENCH SOLDIERS WHO WERE CALLED TO PROTECT THEIR HOMELAND.

And by some accounts it seems that Mr. Poilu preferred to think of himself, and the six or seven men of his squad as *bon hommes*, or simply the good guys.

Below: In 1916 the poilu hung up his old uniform of bright blue tunic and scarlet pants, and donned the new uniform of "horizon blue," as well as his new steel helmet. The helmet wouldn't stop a bullet, but in the trenches it protected against shrapnel wounds.

POILU

Le poilu, or "the hairy one," seems an apt description of the proudly mustached, mud-soaked, and unkempt French fighting man. The word's roots went back to the Napoleonic Wars, and in World War I, some say the word was at first Parisian slang that was soon picked by the press. But it apparently was also an old rustic greeting used by bear-like, rough-and-tumble country folk. And in the French language, **poilu** means animal hair as much as human hair.

MEET MR. POILU

There were at least two 1916 British books named something like, "Meet Mr. Poilu," which characterized Mr. Poilu as a plucky chap, but not quite British. Mr. Poilu was portrayed as demonstrative, with a dramatic temperament, and actually willing to show emotions in victory, or defeat, or anything in between.

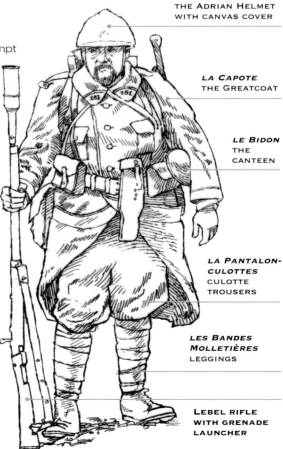

LA CASQUE
THE ADRIAN HELMET
WITH CANVAS COVER

LA CAPOTE
THE GREATCOAT

LE BIDON
THE CANTEEN

LA PANTALON-CULOTTES
CULOTTE TROUSERS

LES BANDES MOLLETIÈRES
LEGGINGS

LEBEL RIFLE
WITH GRENADE
LAUNCHER

RIGHTEOUS WAR

There were many streams of humanity that eventually found themselves on the Western Front facing the *boche*, the despised Germans who were close to imposing another humiliating defeat on the French as they had in 1871. One stream was the men of the Reserve Territorial Army, older men mostly, and then the younger Reserves and the Regulars. Most came from distant farms and villages of the provinces, and spoke the local *patois*. But in the army they all stood together beneath the Tricolor, defending the flag and respecting the traditions of the French Republic. In attempting to expel the foreign invaders, the poilu had no doubt he was on the side of all that was right—or in French *La Guerre du Droit*.

Who were the poilu? They were mostly ordinary civilians who had some previous military training. France had conscription and required its men to serve for three years. Whenever needed, they could be called to back to arms. Since France was primarily an agricultural country, most were farm workers, but there were factory workers and others. There were Parisian roughnecks, graduates of reform school, and even special groups of semi-criminals who were trucked in for raids on the enemy trenches. But mostly it was the good, rural folk of the provinces who occupied the front-line trenches. First and foremost, the poilu were citizens of a great nation, a republic, unlike Britain and Germany, and they were fighting to defend the very existence of their homeland.

More than eight million souls were called upon to save the nation of France, by sacrificing their lives if need be. As historian Alistair Horne points out, this was a time of the unquestioned acceptance of all things just as they were, as well as acceptance of those in control of events. But as the war continued the situation deteriorated. Horne also recognizes that by 1916, the soldiers on the Western Front fought "simply out of a helpless sense of habit, to keep going, to keep alive." After years of immense sacrifice, it was unthinkable to surrender or even think of peace without victory.

REVENGE

EARLY IN THE TWENTIETH CENTURY, MANY FRENCH COMMANDERS BELIEVED THAT IT WAS THE SOLDIER'S WILL TO CONQUER, AND A STRATEGY OF CONSTANT ATTACK, THAT WOULD BE THE WAY TO WIN THE NEXT WAR WITH GERMANY.

The poilu, that bearded, ill-treated, suffering French foot soldier, was, in his millions, his nation's salvation—at the Marne, at Verdun, and throughout the excuciatingly painful Grand Guerre.

The French defeat by Prussia in 1871 had remained a chronic wound for forty years, "not to be spoken of, but never forgotten." "Revanche" was never far from the French consiousness, and a new European war would bring about that revenge.

1914 predictions foresaw a brief and glorious war, concluding in the recapture of the German-held provinces of Alcase and Lorraine. The humiliating French defeat of 1871 would be avenged, and the French soldier would again be supreme in Europe.

As André Maurois writes:

"I went to put on my uniform which my father wanted to see. The Infantry still wore blue tunics and red trousers. Mine had been got out of the wardrobe the day before and smelled of camphor. The puttees felt uncomfortable on my legs. My father looked me over with the severity of an old soldier. 'You must polish up your buttons.' He was sad at my leaving but full of hope for France and happy to see a son of his taking part

in the war of revenge of which he had dreamed since 1871."

And Paul Lintier, in his memoirs, writes of the people's enthusiasm as his artillery unit is about to leave for battle, days after war was declared in August 1914:

"In front of the Toublanc cider-brewery flowers and ribbons in bunches, sprays and cascades carpet the pavement and smother the gun-carriages, ammunition wagons, and limbers. Women and girls arrive with armfuls of hortensias, iris, and roses. Their faces, lit up by the sun and by the excitement of the moment, appear and disappear among the flowers."

The strategy with which the General Staff intended to fight was as quintessentially French as a Zouave's baggy red pantaloons. It was the product of prosperous times, bitter memories, and an imagination as romantic and reckless as a Left Bank poet.

The chef who concocted this deadly stew was Colonel de Grandmaison, Chief of Operations of the General Staff—a man described as a mystic but in time's perspective appears more a mountebank. Grandmaison's doctrine was *élan vital*: It was the will to conquer that would win the day. Reason, prudence, and caution were out the window:

"In the offensive imprudence is the best of assurances...

"Let us go even to excess and that perhaps will not be far enough..."

"From the moment of action every soldier must ardently desire the assault by bayonet as the supreme means of imposing his will upon the enemy and gaining victory..."

"You talk to us of heavy artillery. Thank God, we have none. The strength of the French army is in the lightness of its guns."

(In fact the French 75mm field gun was superb and existed in sufficient numbers. With its highly disciplined, courageous crews, the 75mm was at times France's first and last line of defense and deserves its lasting fame.)

Machine guns were also anathama to Grandmaison; for every St. Étienne machine gun the French possesed, the Germans had ten Maxims. Being complex and essentially defensive in nature, the machine gun was a weapon with very little élan vitale.

The essence of the Grandmaison doctrine was "always attack." Combined with a national mood of belligerence that egotistically ignored German intentions, France rushed toward a debacle in August 1914. Within the first four months of World War I, France would lose 300,000 troops. The grim reality of twentieth-century combat proved that heroism alone was not sufficient for victory. The tragic grandure of the poilu lay in his ability to endure the ceaseless punishment of the modern inferno for four years.

COURAGE

COURAGE AND DETERMINATION
WERE HALLMARKS OF THE FRENCH
SOLDIER IN WWI. THE 1914 ARMY
INSTRUCTION MANUAL ADVISED
THE FRENCH SOLDIER ON HIS
CIVIC DUTY.

PATRIOTISM

Patriotism was part of the unquestioned cultural bedrock of France, and the soldiers of the French army. The soldier was expected to defend, and die if necessary, for the honor of his country. The tricolor flag was more than a symbol; it was an embodiment of the French way of life. As such, the flag was expected to ennoble the fighting spirit of every soldier.

CIVIC DUTY

Every citizen had obligations to the Republic, such as paying taxes. It fell upon the young men to have a special and more profound obligation called the blood tax (conscription). The soldier's job was to defend the Republic, and his regiment, and, if needed, make the ultimate sacrifice.

HONOR

Honor was a near sacred concept in France, both the honor of the French nation, and personal honor. The very act of wearing the splendid uniform of the French army was expected to transform a young man, and fill him with the most noble sentiments. And the greatest honor of all was to defend the glory of France. Also the defense of the reputation of a soldier's regiment was

encouraged in the instruction manual as follows: "The soldier must respect his uniform and the number of his regiment, do everything in his power to emphasize and to give a high opinion of its fine qualities, by his attitude, his courage, and regular and honest conduct."

To continue, "the soldier must love his regiment and consider it as a new family." And, "The camaraderie of the regiment is required; it is a bond that unites men working together for the same cause, running the same dangers, and in virtue of equality, to pay the blood tax to the homeland."

Dénatalité
France had long experienced low birth rates. This translated into a population disadvantage versus Germany. This especially affected the French army, where forty-five-year-old territorial troops were accepted.

FROM A 1914 TRAINING MANUAL

This excerpt illustrates the intense nationalism of much of French culture in the prewar years:

"La Patrie is the Spirit of the French nation.
Our Homeland is the common mother of all the French; it is the source of our laws, our institutions, our habits, our wealth; this is our land, it is our cities, monuments, cemeteries; it includes our noble history, our ancestors, our heroes, our glories, our sorrows; it is the life we lead, our aspirations; it is our honor. Patriotism is the love of our country.

Here within the Fatherland we have everything we need or ever will need! And it is with honor and integrity that we of the Army conduct our lives.

What is the motto of the French army?

Its motto is 'Honor and Fatherland.'

What is our honor?

It's a feeling that includes all actions that are good, just, loyal, and selfless.

What, in particular, is that military honor?

Honor allows the perfect fulfillment of all our soldierly duties, it is bravery in combat, it is the devotion that compels us to rescue comrades in danger; it is finally the cultivation of all loyal and generous sentiments."

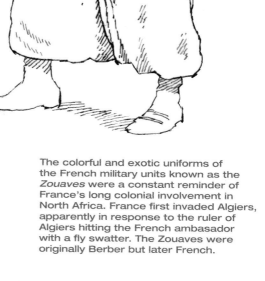

The colorful and exotic uniforms of the French military units known as the *Zouaves* were a constant reminder of France's long colonial involvement in North Africa. France first invaded Algiers, apparently in response to the ruler of Algiers hitting the French ambasador with a fly swatter. The Zouaves were originally Berber but later French.

THE '75 FIELD GUN

THE SOIXANTE-QUINZE WAS DESIGNED FOR OPEN WARFARE AND WAS A BRILLIANT WEAPON. IT WAS THE ANSWER TO THE GERMAN MACHINE GUN AND WOULD BE FRANCE'S SALVATION.

We call it the French '75, but it is the Soixante-Quinze to the French, and to the poilu fighting off the German army, it was simply "Le Faucher" or the Reaper. To us it might seem an unremarkable weapon, but in its day it was a military secret, the first modern gun, and the symbol of French military prowess. With a good crew it could fire up to twenty rounds per minute, perhaps more.

Using the right ammunition it was said to function "like a huge shotgun," each exploding shell spraying 261 deadly balls. A battery of four guns, firing rapidly, could devastate an enemy infantry formation. And this was just the situation that occured in the first weeks of the war.

Like most military equipment early on, the Soixante-Quinze was horse powered. A six-horse team, with another team pulling a caisson loaded with shells, drew each gun. In total the French army could field one thousand batteries in 1914—that's four thousand guns.

Paul Lintier wrote about the French artillery:

"It must be confessed that courage is much easier for us in the artillery than for the foot-soldiers—the least fortunate of all the fighting forces. A gunner under fire is literally unable to run away. The whole battery would see him—his dishonour would be palpable, irretrievable.

Another defeat! Just as in 1870... Just as in 1870! We are all obsessed by the same paralysing thought."

ICONS

EACH ITEM HERE DISPLAYS ONE FACET, AN IRREDUCIBLE NUGGET OF THE LEGEND THAT HAS GROWN UP AROUND LE GRAND GUERRE, THE GREAT WAR. THESE SHORT PARAGRAPHS CAN SERVE AS AN INTRODUCTION TO THE PEOPLE AND COMPLEX PANORAMA OF FRANCE IN THOSE YEARS.

PINARD

Alcohol fortified the fighting spirit and calmed the nerves of the armies in WWI. The Canadians and British had rum, and the Germans had beer. The French had their wine, or **pinard**, as that particular rough army vintage was called. Throughout the war the amount of wine issued varied; in 1918 it was nearly a liter a day. When on a march, the already overburdened poilu somehow managed to carry two canteens: one water and the other wine.

THE KEPI

Perhaps second only to the Eiffel Tower as a symbol of stylish French way of doing things is the **kepi**. That is the round, straight-sided cap with the leather peak, worn by gendarmes, the Foreign Legion, and Claude Rains in the movie *Casablanca*. The kepi might be blue, crimson, or a half dozen other colors depending on the branch of the service. However, for neatness's sake, it was often worn with a light canvas cover. By the end of WWI the kepi was virtually retired from areas of combat.

40

THE SPAD

Guynemer's last airplane was the SPAD. With its smooth clean lines, and undoubted Gallic aesthetic appeal, the SPAD was the very image of an aerial predator. For decades it it would represent the essence of WWI air combat.

Georges Guynemer
It's difficult to remember the many heroes in trench warfare, since it was an affair of mass-man versus the machine. How-ever, France produced fine airplanes, and the air aces who flew them became beloved national celebrities. None surpassed Georges Guynemer, frail, tubercular, and with fifty-three victories.

CHAR RENAULT TANK

The FT-17 was the first tank to wield a cannon in a swiveling turret. It was small, so it was hard to target, and advancing troops felt safe using it as rolling cover. It was agile and robust, and when traveling in swarms, it overwhelmed enemy trenches. And maybe most important, by 1918 there were thousands of them available. With the FT-17, a weapon had at last been created that made trench warfare obsolete.

MITRAILLEUSE

THE ORIGINAL MITRAILLEUSE WAS A TOP-SECRET 38 BARREL GATLING-LIKE GUN. IT WAS USED IN THE FRANCO-PRUSSIAN WAR AND IT WAS CONSIDERED EFFECTIVE. HOWEVER, IT WAS SO SECRET THAT TOO FEW GUN CREWS HAD BEEN TRAINED FOR ITS USE IN COMBAT. THOUGH DESPERATELY NEEDED, GUNS STOOD UNUSED FOR WANT OF OPERATORS.

ammunition magazine was open, and could be easily clogged with dirt, and apparently the manufacture was substandard. However, the Chauchat was used throughout the war. It was the first light machine gun, and even German troops, being without such a weapon, used captured Chauchats. It was eventually issued to American troops, although the U.S. had developed the far superior Browning Automatic Rifle.

DESIGNED BY COLONEL CHAUCHAT, THE FRENCH ARMY CALLED IT THE "MACHINE RIFLE 1915"

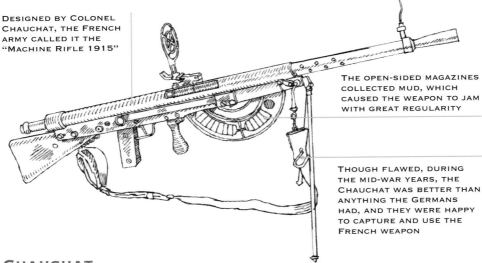

THE OPEN-SIDED MAGAZINES COLLECTED MUD, WHICH CAUSED THE WEAPON TO JAM WITH GREAT REGULARITY

THOUGH FLAWED, DURING THE MID-WAR YEARS, THE CHAUCHAT WAS BETTER THAN ANYTHING THE GERMANS HAD, AND THEY WERE HAPPY TO CAPTURE AND USE THE FRENCH WEAPON

CHAUCHAT

A light portable machine gun was needed, a weapon that could be fired from the trenches, or while approaching the enemy in an attack across no-man's-land. The **Chauchat** was the French army's choice. The basic idea was ready, being based on prototypes designed before the war. But unfortunately it turned out to be a flawed design, some say it was the worst firearm ever created. The

THE HOTCHKISS

The Hotchkiss Company's Mle 1914 was the primary French machine gun in the war, and would be for the next twenty years. It was efficient because it was air-cooled. It didn't need constant water refills for cooling, like the British Vickers or German Maxim. And, being air-cooled, it didn't emit a cloud of steam that might betray a machine gun's position. The generals were right when they said machine guns were defensive weapons. The Hotchkiss was

Above: The St. Etienne Mle 1907 was another machine gun used early in the war. It was later replaced by the more reliable Hotchkiss.

a heavy 155 pounds. But to conform to the Armée de Terre's doctrine of élan vital, a vintage film shows a three-man team running across no-man's-land with the rest of the troops, then stopping and setting up a Hotchkiss in fewer than thirty seconds. It all looks so simple.

AVIATION

MILITARY AIRCRAFT WERE CONSTANTLY IN OPERATION ABOVE THE FRONT LINE. WHEN THEY CRASHED, THE TROOPS RUSHED IN TO PICK UP THE PIECES.

One of the top French aces was Georges Guynemer. He was a frail young man, with an aristocratic manner and a love of science and engineering. He shot down more than fifty enemy planes and become a national hero. One day in 1917 he failed to return from a mission, and the French nation grieved. It is said that in the evenings, mothers told their children that Guynemer had merely flown far away, never to return.

Shown here is a Morane-Saulnier fighter aircraft, a type Guynemer flew, though he favored the Nieuport, and the SPAD.

The elegant dark blue uniform set aviators apart.

Lieutenant-Colonel Maillard, commanding the 238th Infantry, said to Corporal Pilot Guynemer, "Well done."

In a note to the Lieutenant-Colonel, the officers, and the whole regiment he wrote,

> "Having witnessed the aerial attack you made upon a German Aviatik over their trenches, I applaud your victory, which terminated in the vertical fall of your adversary. We offer you warmest congratulations, and share the joy you must have felt in achieving so brilliant a success."

Parts of a Voisin Biplane

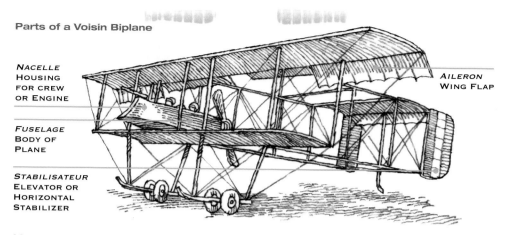

NACELLE HOUSING FOR CREW OR ENGINE

AILERON WING FLAP

FUSELAGE BODY OF PLANE

STABILISATEUR ELEVATOR OR HORIZONTAL STABILIZER

Many aviation words come from WWI-era France, and are still in use.

OLD CHARLES

Another time infantrymen had observed two falling airplanes. The French plane reached the earth just before its pilot's last victim fell also, in flames. The soldiers pitied the poor victor, who had not, as they thought, survived his conquest! They rushed to his aid, expecting to pick him up crushed to atoms. But Guynemer stood up without aid. He seemed like a ghost; but he was standing, he was alive, and the excited soldiers took hold of him and carried him off in triumph. A general of the division soon approached, and immediately ordered the troops to give a military salute for the victor.

Guynemer called his personal SPAD "Vieux Charles," or Old Charles.

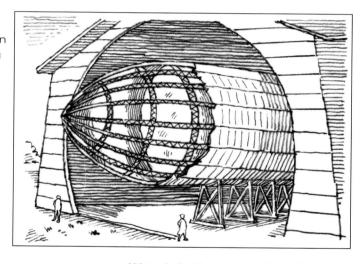

Although the French operated a few airships during the war, they were dated, and lacked the speed and the rigid construction of German zeppelins. Also, French troops sometimes fired at and once shot down their own airships. Observation planes were essential for spotting artillery targets. These slow planes were guarded by faster pursuit planes.

TRENCH ARGOT

A SELECTION OF EVEN MORE VOCABULARY WORDS FROM *L'ARGOT DES TRANCHÉES*, THAT SPECIAL LANGUAGE, FOR AND BY, THE MILLIONS OF ORDINARY MEN MAROONED BY CIRCUMSTANCES FAR FROM HOME.

TALKING TRENCH

La Bochie: *la Bochie* was the term for Germany, and a German was a *boche*.

Un Boyau: The entrance to a trench, original meaning "a gut."

Un Cerf: a skilled cavalryman and his horse were "a deer."

Le Groin de Cochon: a gas mask, and it looked like a pig's snout.

Les Pompes: soldier's boots; the "pump" is an old name for certain shoes; going up and down like a pump-piston might be the word origin.

Villages Détruits
The back and forth of battle had put many villages in the line of fire. Some were utterly destroyed, and after the war it was decided not to rebuild them. These were the *villages détruits*, or destroyed villages, and many were in the vicinity of Verdun. After the war, a Red Zone was created because of dangerous unexploded munitions. The government declared that "these were the villages that had died for France."

SYSTEM D

Life in the trenches was tough, and often to survive, the poilu followed the path of least resistance, or just improvised. He found a method of judiciously cutting corners, disappearing at the right moment to avoid responsibility, and looking the other way when someone else did the same thing. **System D** was the French version of just muddling through. And it was a way of life that consumed the mind of the **le lapin**, the clever, brave soldier. In practice this might consist of scrapping out a personal dugout in a not quite

The Caquot

Armies had used observation balloons from at least the time of the Civil War. But Lt. Caquot had created a new design, like a streamlined sausage (thus winning the name "saucisse"), with three rear fins for stabilization. They were valuable for artillery spotting, but conspicuous, and fairly easy targets for enemy planes or anti-aircraft guns. The crews did have parachutes, and there were techniques for coming down quickly, but it was dangerous work. The expected life span for these balloons was two weeks, and some came down in hours.

approved area, or finding some food, or a pair of shoes from who-knows-where. It was really a way to make a creaky and complex system function.

THE TOMB OF COUPERIN

The famous French composer Maurice Ravel, like many other Frenchmen, was consumed by a patriotic need to serve his country. Too frail for the army, Ravel became an accomplished truck driver, and specialized in rescuing abandoned trucks on the road to Verdun. For most of his route he was within the range of enemy guns, and he drove day and night overloaded on treacherous roads. His own wartime adventure was when once his favorite truck, which he named Adelaide, broke down and became lost in a dangerous wood, and it was ten days before Adelaide could be retrieved. Despite this demanding work, he continued composing during the war years, producing his great *Le Tombeau de Couperin*, dedicated to friends who had been killed in the war.

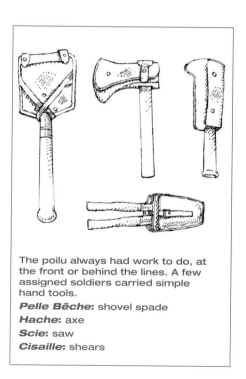

The poilu always had work to do, at the front or behind the lines. A few assigned soldiers carried simple hand tools.

Pelle Bêche: shovel spade
Hache: axe
Scie: saw
Cisaille: shears

SOUP

ABOVE: *GAMELLE INDIVIDUELLE* OR MESS KIT

THE SOLDIER'S TROUGH

Troops on the march might camp at a farm or village and be required to use their own cooking skills. Usually there was a good cook in the platoon who could find a hen and make a feast.

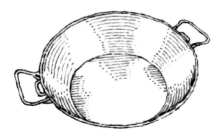

The cooking gear the army provided consisted of the mess kit, or the 1852 **gamelle individuelle**. And there was also a large metal dish for food preparation for four, called the **plat à quatre**.

Two other much-heard words were **la becquetance**, meaning soldier's grub, and **une auge**, literally a trough, but meaning a soldier's plate.

THE COOK

The great diarist Corporal Louis Barthas always had great praise for the brave cooks and food carriers who stood by their kitchens in the midst of enemy bombardment. Even so, there were times of hunger. When troops were transported by rail, in freight cars, every human amenity was lacking. It was only their own food, the scraps of bread and cheese stuffed into shoulder bags, that sustained them.

For the exhausted poilu in the field, deprived of all civilian comfort, the greatest gifts were a "good fire, a good bed, and a good meal." And on occasion, to nourish the spirit, a view of a "resplendent, radiant, silvery moon."

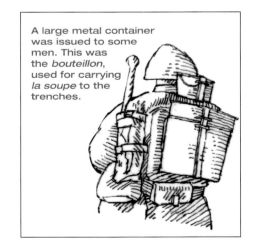

A large metal container was issued to some men. This was the *bouteillon*, used for carrying *la soupe* to the trenches.

Menu
A Taste of the Trenches

P.D.D.M. (Petit Déjeuner Du Matin)
Early Morning Breakfast
Coffee (Jus), Bread, Wine, Leftovers from Dinner

La Soupe
10:00 A.M....(The Corporal Will Distribute)
Ratatouille, or Common French Ragout with Canned Meat,
called "Monkey Meat"
(navy beans, potatoes, rice, carrots, red wine,
chocolate, etc.)

Other Entrees when available
Salt Pork Ragout
Meat and Bean Hash
Lard (in place of meat)

Dinner
5:00 P.M....Breakfast Leftovers

Evening
Rabioter (leftovers again)
Rab may be provided by nimble fingers at
the Quartermaster's stores

Water purified with hypochlorite and sodium chlorate
Coffee is always available
Try Our Bread
Our specialty is over cooking

ROLLERS

WITH ENEMY SHELLING AND SNIPER FIRE, THE FOOD THAT DID MAKE IT TO THE TRENCHES WAS COLD, AND MIGHT CONTAIN SPLASHES OF MUD; HOWEVER, IT WAS THE BEST THAT COULD BE DONE CONSIDERING THE CIRCUMSTANCES.

Early in the war, small groups of men were expected to prepare their own meals. Beginning in 1915 each company of two hundred men was to get its own wheeled field kitchen. These were known as *roulantes* or **rollers**, and they largely made soldiers' cooking fires obsolete. The rollers were efficient, and cooks used whatever was available for making their stews. The trick as always

was to get hot food to the troops up front. The field kitchen shown had been captured from the Germans.

Two food carriers or *les hommes de la soupe* carried a huge container of prepared food between them, and sometimes strapped on dozens of filled canteens. Since water needed to be decontaminated, from the health viewpoint it was often smarter to drink wine.

It was dangerous getting to the trenches, and once there the simplest activity might prove fatal. The enemy might see smoke from a fire, so using the flame of a candle was a good way to heat coffee.

MONKEY MEAT

The army had a Standard Ration plan, to provide two good meals a day, with meat, vegetables, and desserts. And that worked well for behind the line troops seated at a table. A soldier entering the front lines was supplied with rations for two days, placed in a mess tin or shoulder bags. After that he depended on food sent up from the field kitchens. He also carried Reserve Rations, or *Vivres de Resérve*. This included the infamous canned meat from Madagascar, which the poilu called *singe* or **monkey meat**. There were also hard biscuits, and packets of dried soup and coffee, with sugar, a rare commodity at the time. The Standard Ration changed over the years according to availability. From 1915 onward, pork was the army's meat

of choice. Importing beef cattle from overseas become risky because of submarine warfare. Beans and lentils were favored vegetables, and it is said the poilu rejected rice, which was new to the French palate.

TRENCH LANGUAGE

IT'S BEEN SAID THAT THE FRENCH SOLDIER HAD THE RICHEST TRENCH-TALK VOCABULARY ON THE WESTERN FRONT. YOU DON'T EVEN HAVE TO SPEAK FRENCH TO GET THE MEANING OF THE WORDS.

Artillery shells were often given names based on visual characteristics, such as *un pernod*, after its smoke, green like the drink, or the black smoke of *un gros noir*. There were others like "zimboum" and "zinzin" that mimicked the sound of passing shells.

THE ADRIAN HELMET

The French steel helmet was designed by Intendant-General August-Louis Adrian, and was patterned after the Paris fireman's helmet. It was called the M15 Adrian Helmet. The design features long, smooth curves, and has an unmistakable French style. However in the field, the helmet had its faults. It was made of a thin gauge of steel, and provided only moderate protection on the battlefield, unlike the British helmet, which at times could stop a bullet. But it was adequate protection for shrapnel, and stones kicked up by bursting shells. It was also nicknamed **la cloche**, the bell, and became the fashion template for a generation of ladies' hats.

The small military cup is le quart, a big stewpot is a marmite, and *le Moulin a café* is a coffee grinder, yet another name for the machine gun.

The thin, fencing sword-like French bayonet was named "Rosalie" after a popular song of 1914. The sheet music for the song is illustrated with a picture of a trooper on a battlefield, holding his Lebel rifle with attached bayonet. This apparently is the association between the bayonet and the song. The bayonet actually had several other, less romantic-sounding names, such as the "fork" and the "toothpick," as well as the fearsome *le tire-boche* or Boche-screw. The Germans, in turn, called the thin bayonet "the knitting needle."

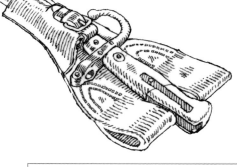

The evocative French trench lexicon include the following words.

Le séchoir: clothes line the barbed wire in no-man's-land just beyond the French trench line where the bodies of dead soldiers would hang

le sac a terre: sandbag

le Machine à Découdre: the un-sewing machine The machine gun that could rip any-thing, or anyone to pieces

Ila Commotion: Shell-shock

le Flingue: the rifle, or gun

le Bidasse: messmate

le Fanfaron: scoundrel

Livret Individuel: paybook

le Biffin: looking like a rag picker

le coupe de main: raid, raid in force

l'aero: airplane

le Gaz: gas

schrapnells: undercooked peas or beans

le danse: the fight

The WW1 soldier's body and clothing were an ideal home for insect pests including:

le got (the flea), *le toto* (the louse), and *le puce* (all insect pests). The communal shirt-hunt was one way to combat an infestation.

INFANTRY

THERE WERE WORDS IN THE POILU LEXICON TO DESCRIBE EVERY TYPE OF FELLOW SOLDIER, FROM SLACKERS TO HEROES, FROM RABBITS TO DUCKS.

INFANTRY SOLDIER

Fantassin was the name given to the French infantry soldier. The notion of infant or child is associated with both the French and English word. And the army, just as the family, prized obedience above all else.

RABBIT

Lapin, or rabbit, was a term for the good soldier. Like the rabbit, the good soldier must be fast, agile, and live by his wits. Fearing for its life, the rabbit was known to play dead, and at times a poilu might be well advised to do the same. The rabbit also burrows into earthen holes for safety.

POILU PRIVILEGE

To be accurate, the name *poilu* did not apply to every French soldier. After a newcomer had experienced his first shelling in a frontline trench, or had survived combat, he had earned the privilege of being called a *poilu*. This was an exclusive community, and likely to be short lived, since 26% of frontline troops were killed in combat.

BAD SOLDIER

The word **péteux** names carelessness and laziness as two traits of the bad soldier. It took constant effort to repair broken trenches and maintain some level of cleanliness in the overpowering and then barely noticed filth of trench life. And with enemy observation planes overhead, the careful soldier avoided being too active during daylight hours. The noisy soldier was a very bad soldier, since he invited a volley of enemy mortar fire.

DUCK

How appropriate it seems to use "duck" (**canard**), as a slang word for sniper, popping up above camouflage or the top of the trench, taking a quick shot, and then down again. However, most snipers were hidden, silent, and motionless, waiting for an inexperienced enemy soldier who forgot to keep his head down.

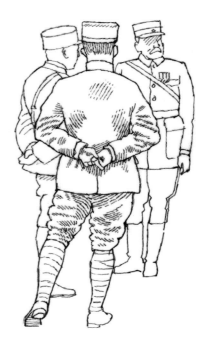

THEM

Throughout the war years more than eight million men wore the horizon blue uniform of the French army. Many were never ordered to the front lines. The word **ceux** (or them) was used somewhat derisively for these lucky, or pampered, rear echelon troops.

ATTACK/ COUNTERATTACK

It took only a few days of warfare for the French General Staff's Plan XVII to fail with dire consequences.

"It takes a charging force of infantry six minutes to run a thousand yards, where a musket would get in three shots, a modern rifle would put in from 180 to 300 shots, and would be firing almost continuously."

An old hand speaking to a would-be volunteer:

"With continuous work eight hours a day, it takes at least two years to make a real soldier. You don't know how to use a single weapon. You couldn't fix a bayonet. You don't know the workings of a Lebel rifle."

MODERN WAR

The dream of a quick thrust, victory, and a speedy end to fighting soon evaporated. Quoting a contemporary account:

"Retreat amid the wounded, retreat in hopeless rear-guard actions with dead on every side, retreat on roads crowded with homeless and hopeless refugees fleeing anywhere away from the advancing horror of war, retreat without food, retreat without sleep, retreat in rain, in mud, in blazing heat, in choking thirst, retreat under the reproachful eyes of deserted women, retreat under the stinging shame of defeat, retreat until the heart was as weary as the feet, and death would be a gift. Retreat over a front of 200 miles, with every road, every street, every lane, every by-path surging with misery, crowded with panic."

In this, the First Battle of the Marne, the enemy was only a few miles from Paris. Their battle plan was working, and observation planes helped the effective German artillery.

"Vast stores of supplies were being hurried in for use in the event of a siege. Enormous herds of cattle were being driven into Paris to graze on the waste spaces kept free of buildings, not to interfere with the fire of the inner forts. A steady stream of people had their faces turned to the southwest, women and children escaping from the threat of war, trekking for distant points of safety, with their goods piled into the bullock carts of the peasant, the pony carriages of the rich, or even in wheelbarrows. In almost every group there were tiny children and babies."

THE MIRACLE OF THE MARNE

The German advance was so quick, supplies couldn't keep up. French forces regrouped, most notably with the assistance of Parisian buses and taxicabs.

"Four thousand taxis, motor-busses and motor-cars were speeding from Paris to the front. Men rode on the front, on the back and hung on to the springs. Twelve and fourteen men piled into and on a taxicab. The motorbusses carried sixty and seventy, men hanging on by the straps of their rifles, jammed into window frames. They looked like insects on a plant. Inside they were packed like herrings in a cask. But they roared with delight at taking a taxi to the front. By noon, General Manoury's army had been reinforced by 70,000 troops."

VERDUN

IF THE BATTLE OF THE MARNE SAVED FRANCE AS A NATION, IT WAS THE BATTLE OF VERDUN THAT SAVED THE BELEAGUERED SPIRIT OF FRANCE.

DOUAUMONT

The Germans planned a massive attack on the ancient fortress city of Verdun. When the French armies responded, the Germans hoped to annihilate them. The titanic Battle of Verdun raged from February 1916 until December, and there were nearly a million casualties on both sides. The thick walls of the fortress were leveled as if by an earthquake, and the battleground was a moonscape. The massive fortress of Douaumont was lost, and then retaken. But France was not defeated, and Verdun became a symbol of heroic resistance. In fact with conditions so wretched there, the fighting had descended into dazed and desperate savagery. Trench warfare could be civilized when compared to Verdun. And it was at Verdun that the Germans first introduced the flame-thrower and phosgene gas.

WE DO NOT PASS!

"They Shall Not Pass"...meaning France, Verdun, would be defended to the last inch, by the last man. The credit for these immortal words usually goes to General Nivelle. It was in June of 1916, and the battle had been going on for five months, and both Mort Homme hill and Fort Vaux had fallen. The phrase became popular, and was famously used on patriotic posters. In the 1930s, it was the anti-fascist slogan.

Fort Douaumont was an imposing structure. It was rather new and had been modernized in 1913, and declared indestructible. In the battle a tiny garrison of 57 men finally guarded it. The fort was conquered without a shot, the Germans entering through an unguarded passageway.

SACRED WAY

With major rail lines interrupted, this 45 mile long road, then known as *La Route*, was the vital supply lifeline to Verdun. With great foresight in 1915, the road had been widened and improved to handle two lanes of truck traffic. With Verdun under siege, substantial efforts were made to keep *La Route* operating. This included seven squadrons of fighters to defend against German planes. Most important were the thousands of men who directed traffic flow, and serviced broken-down vehicles. Trucks that caused traffic jams were immediately hauled off the road, and dozens of repair trucks were available for quick fixes. Cargo and troop trucks drove day and night, especially providing the artillery and ammunition in short supply at Verdun. The name *Voie Sacrée* (sacred way) was applied after the war, and today the modernized road called RD1916 is maintained as a national monument.

To maintain morale, units were rotated in and out of Verdun. Especially prominent were colonial troops, including Moroccan soldiers.

ALAN SEEGER

ALAN SEEGER WAS A REMARKABLE YOUNG AMERICAN. HE WAS A HARVARD GRADUATE, A SOMETIME BOHEMIAN, AND AN EDITOR AND JOURNALIST. HE HAD BEEN LIVING IN FRANCE WHEN THE WAR BROKE OUT. PASSIONATELY EMBRACING FRENCH CULTURE, HE JOINED THE FRENCH ARMY. THE CLARITY OF DESCRIPTION OF THE WAR IN HIS DIARY AND LETTERS IS UNSURPASSED. SEEGER DIED IN BATTLE ON JULY 4, 1916.

Alan Seeger was the uncle of folk singer Pete Seeger.

"September 24.—We are to attack tomorrow morning....I am very confident and sanguine about the result and expect to march right up to the Aisne, borne on in an irresistible *élan*. I have been waiting for this moment for more than a year. It will be the greatest moment in my life. I shall take good care to live up to it.

October 25, 1915, Letter to His Mother

The part we played in the battle is briefly as follows. We broke camp about 11 o'clock the night of the 24th, and marched up through ruined Souain to our place in one of the numerous *boyaux* where the troupes d'attaque were massed. The cannonade was pretty violent all that night, as it had been for several days previous, but toward dawn it reached an intensity unimaginable to anyone who has not seen a modern battle. A little before 9.15 the fire lessened suddenly and the crackle of the fusillade between the reports of the cannon told us that the first wave of assault had left and the attack begun. At the same time we received the order to advance. The German artillery had now begun to open upon us in earnest. Amid the most infernal roar of every kind of fire-arms and through an atmosphere heavy with dust and smoke, we marched up through the *boyaux* to the *tranchées de départ*. At shallow places and over breaches that shells had made in the bank we caught momentary glimpses of the blue lines sweeping up the hillside or silhouetted on the crest where they poured into the German trenches. When the last wave of the Colonial brigade had left, we followed. *Baïonnette au canon*, in lines of *tirailleurs* (riflemen), we crossed the open space between the lines, over the barbed wire, where not so many of our men were lying as I had feared (thanks to the efficacy of the bombardment) and over the German trench, knocked to pieces and filled with their dead. In some places they still resisted in isolated groups. Opposite us, all was over, and the herds of prisoners were being already led down as we went up. We cheered, more in triumph than in hate, but the poor devils, terror-stricken, held up their hands, begged for their lives, cried 'Kamerad,' '*Bon Français*,' even '*Vive la France*.' We advanced and lay down in columns by two behind the second crest. Meanwhile, bridges had been thrown across trenches and boyaux, and the artillery, leaving the emplacements where they had been anchored a whole year, came across and took position in the open, a magnificent spectacle. Squadrons of cavalry came up. Suddenly the long, unpicturesque guerre de tranchées was at an end and the field really presented the aspect of the familiar battle pictures—the battalions in manoeuvre, the officers, superbly indifferent to danger, galloping about on their chargers. But now the German guns, moved back, began to get our range and the shells to burst over and around batteries and troops, many with admirable precision. Here my best comrade was struck down by shrapnel at my side—painfully but not mortally wounded.

That night we spent in the rain. With portable picks and shovels each man dug himself in as well as possible. The next day our concentrated artillery again began the bombardment, and again the fusillade announced the entrance of the infantry into action. But this time only the wounded appeared coming back, no prisoners. I went out and gave water to one of these, eager to get news. It was a young soldier, wounded in the hand. His face and voice bespoke the emotion of the experience he had been through in a way that I will never forget. '*Ah, les salauds!*' he cried, 'They let us come right up to the barbed wire without firing. Then a hail of grenades and balls. My comrade fell, shot through the leg, got up, and the next moment had his head taken off by a grenade before my eyes.' 'And the barbed wire, wasn't it cut down by the bombardment?' 'Not at all in front of us.' I congratulated him

on having a *blessure heureuse* (happy injury) and being well out of the affair. But he thought only of his comrade and went on down the road toward Souain, nursing his mangled hand, with the stream of wounded seeking their *postes de secours* (First Aid posts).

The afternoon of the 28th should have been our turn. We had spent four days under an almost continual bombardment. The regiment had been decimated, though many of us had not fired a shot. After four such days as I hope never to repeat, under the strain of sitting inactive, listening to the slow whistle of 210-millimetre shells as they arrived and burst more or less in one's proximity, it was a real relief to put *sac au dos* (backpack) and go forward. We marched along in columns by two, behind a crest, then over and across an exposed space under the fire of their 77's. That cost us some men, and took formation to attack on the border of a wood, somewhere behind which they were entrenched. And here we had a piece of luck. For our colonel, a soldier of the old school, stronger for honor than expediency, had been wounded in the first days of the action. Had he been in command, we all think that we should have been sent into the wood (and we would have gone with *élan*) notwithstanding that the 1er Etranger had just attacked gallantly but unsuccessfully and had been badly cut up. The commandant of our battalion, who had succeeded him in command, when he heard, after a reconnaissance, that the wire had not been sufficiently cut, refused to risk his regiment. So you have him to thank."

TRIAGE

EARLY ON A ROUGH SYSTEM FOR
PRIORITY CARE ALREADY EXISTED,
BUT IT NEEDED TO BE EXPANDED.
THE SYSTEM WAS CALLED TRIAGE,
AND IT MEANT THAT THOSE WHO
MOST NEEDED HELP, AND WERE
EXPECTED TO SURVIVE, WERE
TREATED FIRST.

Removing the injured from narrow
trenches was difficult, and usually
too tight for a normal stretcher.
Soldiers were issued lengths of
canvas to place under the injured
and to use like a hammock to carry
the wounded to safety.

THE WALKING WOUNDED

The Sanitary Service knew that the
trenches of the Western Front were cut
into ancient farmland that for centuries
had been enriched with manure. Add
to that the muck of far from pristine
trench life, and even the most superficial
wound might become deadly. There
were injuries of every sort, but head
injuries from exploding shells were
common, along with mangled feet from
grenades thrown into trenches. Medical
attention given less than an hour after
injury, the Golden Hour, could be the
difference between life and death.
The *petite blessé* were the walking-
wounded.

Often it was the *Brancardiers* or stretcher-bearers who snatched the wounded from the battlefield, strapped them onto wheeled stretchers called "brouettes," and pushed them to the nearest aid station, or *Post Secour*.

Hundreds of Americans, many from Ivy League colleges, volunteered to drive ambulances for the French army. The most notable, if not legendary group, was the American Field Service. Applicants were required to have a cool head, and a good grasp of the French language. Also needed was the ability to maneuver a Model T ambulance over shell-torn roads at night without headlights, and always in the rain, or so it seemed. The Model T ambulance was the jeep of WWI; it was rugged, capable; it held three stretcher cases; and it arrived from America, disassembled, in large wooden crates.

HOLDING

TENIR MIGHT BE DEFINED IN TWO WAYS; ORIGINALLY IT MEANT "HOLD THE POSITION AT ALL COSTS." BUT AS OF 1917 IT MEANT "JUST HOLD YOURSELF TOGETHER, UNTIL THERE'S A CHANGE FOR THE BETTER."

THE COCKROACH

Many *poilu* came from rural backgrounds and had been comfortable with accepting orders. These *poilu* would never think of raising their voices in protest, so they never complained.

For some the flame of patriotism still burned bright. *Jusqu'au bout* was their motto, or, "to the end, no matter what it takes." For the rest it was a shrug of the shoulders and a distant gaze. There was no hope left, and that was *la cafard*: simply depression. To be completely literal, *la cafard* was the cockroach.

The journalist Herbert Ward describes the desolate scene after a battle. "We passed many heaps of broken rifles, the detached barrels bent into curious shapes, and many of the stocks splintered to fragments by bullets. Strangely dramatic I found

Above: French soldiers congregate in a huge shell hole during the Nivelle Offensive in April 1917. The huge French/British operation named the Nivelle Offensive was supposed to end the war in 1917. Instead it nearly ended the French army. Within two weeks France suffered 118,000 casualties and 28,000 deaths. This disaster led to mutinies that spread to at least 40,000 French soldiers and in some way touched half the army.

these heaps of broken weapons; mere wreckage in themselves, but how they make one think! It surely does not require any unusual gift of imagination to feel that in those very piles of distorted fragments is the whole tragic story of human strife: courage, despair, and death."

After General Nivelle's failed attempt at ending the war, the élan of the *poilu* was broken. Some units refused to return to the front; frontline units refused to attack. Officers were disobeyed. But the poilu, still patriotic, continued to man the trenches, ready and willing to repel any enemy attack.

This was a time to rebuild the French army. General Pétain wisely made changes: cleaner barracks, better food, and a fair system of furloughs. The army began to heal. In 1918 when Pétain's "tanks and Americans" were available, the poilu was again ready to confront the enemy. The solidarity of France was safe; the "Union Sacrée" would hold.

PEACE

In October 1918 the Germans asked for an armistice; still, a whirlwind of Allied assaults continued throughout the month. Finally the French and Germans signed the armistice document in a rail car and the fighting ended abruptly and unexpectedly on Nov. 11, at 11 A.M., this was the never-to-be-forgotten 11/11/11.

At times during the war, fields of blue cornflower had grown between the lines of trenches. And it was these flowers, the bluet, that were remembered, and began to stand for France's wartime sacrifices, much like the American and British red poppy.

AUGUSTIN TREBUCHON

The artillery continued throughout the morning. Allied Supreme Commander Foch said that he "wanted to pursue the Germans until the final moment." It is also said that artillery crews fired until the very end, so they could claim to have fired the last shot of the war. Then at the appointed time, there was quiet.

Corporal Bartha's diary records:

"And now this forever immortal day has arrived! This happiness, this joy, overwhelmed us. We couldn't keep it in our hearts. We stood there looking at each other, mute and stupid."

But there were other tragic stories on Armistice Day. Nearly three thousand men died on the last day of the war. The French messenger Augustin Trebuchon was killed only ten minutes before eleven. He held a note for his comrades saying "Assemble at 11:30 for hot soup."

French and British prisoners, released from Germany, walking from Mabham (50 kilometers) to the headquarters of the Eighty-Ninth Division at Tailly, Meuse. On the Laneuville-sur-Meuse-Beauclair Road, Meuse, France. November 15, 1918.

"TOMMY WAS THE DOGGED TROOPER IN THE TRENCHES OF THE WESTERN FRONT."

CHAPTER THREE

BRITAIN WITH THE TOMMY

TOMMY ATKINS

TOMMY ATKINS IS THE NAME LONG
ASSOCIATED WITH THE BRITISH
SOLDIER. DURING THE GLORY
DAYS OF EMPIRE, TOMMY WAS
THE TOUGH PROFESSIONAL WHO
IMPLEMENTED PAX BRITANNIA
IN BRITISH COLONIES AROUND
THE WORLD. AND IN WORLD
WAR I, TOMMY WAS THE DOGGED
TROOPER IN THE TRENCHES OF THE
WESTERN FRONT.

the world. The bloody South African or Boer War of 1900 had forced the British to confront something like modern warfare. But a lesson had been learned.

When war was declared on August 4, 1914, the small, all-volunteer British army was ready to quickly cross the English Channel and take on the large German army. This was the BEF, the British Expeditionary Force.

TOMMY

The Tommy of 1900 was working class, born-and-bred; although often it was lack of work that led a young man to visit the recruiting sergeant. Yes, the army life was not without danger, but civilian factories and mines also took a toll of injuries and death. In 1913 a Welsh mine explosion killed more than four hundred men. Upon signing, for seven years, the army offered steady paid work, and a chance to see the world, and Tommy knew where his next meal was coming from. But clearly it was not an easy life. And an off-duty Tommy could be a troublemaker; he liked his beer, and the ladies, as well as a friendly tavern brawl.

THE REGULAR ARMY

Compared to the huge European forces, the British army was tiny, around 300,000 men, with half that number garrisoned in British possessions around the world. It was, however, well trained and disciplined, and it boasted that its riflemen were crack shots, the best in

THE OLD CONTEMPTIBLES

Hoping for a quick victory against the French, Germany had not expected Britain to enter the war. The story goes that the kaiser had derisively called the British force "that contemptible little army." Far from ineffective, the British fought with great heroism, notably using massed rifle fire to stop a German attack at the Battle of Mons. With grim humor, British troops would later refer to themselves as "the old contemptibles."

TOMMY 1917

As the war continued, Britain assembled a vast army. Patriotic calls were made for volunteers, and hundreds of thousands responded. Finally conscription was begun in 1916 to replace continuing heavy losses. So now Tommy was no longer a separate, and only sometimes useful, species of fighting men; it could be just about anybody. Every category of social class was represented. There was the working- or middle-class Tommy, the fit or undernourished Tommy, and there were even Bantam Battalions for the smaller Tommy who might measure in at five feet tall or so. And from the beginning, as far as outsiders were concerned, Empire troops from Canada, Australia, New Zealand, and South Africa were also called Tommy.

THE THICK WOOLEN 1902 PATTERN SERVICE DRESS KHAKI UNIFORMS WERE WARM IN THE WINTER, AND UNCOMFORTABLE AND SCRATCHY IN THE SUMMER

THE RIFLE SLING, AS WELL AS THE BELT AND POUCHES, WERE COTTON WEBBING. LEATHER HAD BEEN PHASED OUT IN 1908

ATTACHED TO THE BAYONET SCABBARD WAS THE WOODEN HANDLE FOR THE ENTRENCHING TOOL

ICONS

IT'S NOT UNUSUAL FOR RELICS FROM PAST TIMES TO ENGAGE US AND EXCITE OUR IMAGINATION. BUT IT IS THOSE FEW ITEMS THAT CONTINUE TO ATTRACT US, WHILE SUMMING UP THE ESSENCE OF AN ERA, THAT BECOME ICONS.

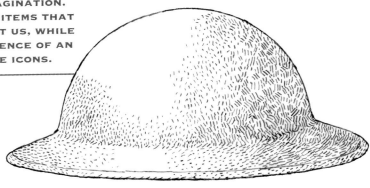

THE BRODIE

It was called the **tin hat**, **wash basin**, **battle bowler**, while officially termed the "Helmet, Steel, Mk I." Few objects had as many informal names. The one that stuck was **"Brodie helmet,"** after inventor John Brodie's 1915 design. It was a shallow hat with a wide brim made of tough manganese steel. The helmet was a rugged personal umbrella for troops huddling in the trenches. The Brodie could deflect an overhead rain of shrapnel balls, as well as debris hurled about by exploding shells. The steel helmet was a rare item in 1915, and remained permanently in the trenches, passed on from one outfit to the next. By 1916 every Tommy had one of this own.

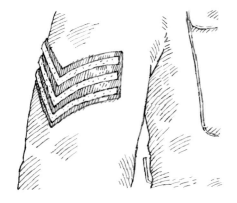

Big downward-pointing chevrons are the classic British insignia of rank for sergeants, corporals, and lance corporals—the latter rank being just below corporal, and requiring some degree of leadership ability. The rank is also known as the **lance jack**, and tracing word origins, the lance refers to an experienced medieval spear-carrier. Shown here are sergeant's stripes; the lance jack had a single chevron.

THE REGULATION MUSTACHE

Up until 1916 army regulations required troops to sport a mustache. A fierce mustache would supposedly allow a British soldier to command respect among bearded colonial subjects. Its greatest exponent was the heroic Lord Kitchener, of recruiting poster fame.

The London Bobby's whistle found its way into the trenches. The shrill, penetrating sound of the trench whistle communicated officer's commands to troops in the midst of chaos and noise. By far the best-known piped order was the signal to go over the top.

Uncle Charlie was the order to march with full equipment, a burden weighing in at 66 lbs. or so. A lesser load, more appropriate for an attack in no-man's-land, is shown here:

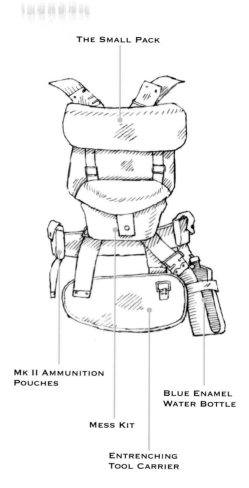

THE SMALL PACK

MK II AMMUNITION POUCHES

MESS KIT

ENTRENCHING TOOL CARRIER

BLUE ENAMEL WATER BOTTLE

URDU AND HINDI

WITH A STRONG PRESENCE IN INDIA AND ENVIRONS FOR ONE HUNDRED YEARS, TOMMY'S EVERYDAY SPEECH APPROPRIATED MANY WORDS FROM THE LOCAL VOCABULARY.

KHAKI

Easily the most famous Asian word adopted by the British army is **khaki**. Variants are found in both Persian and Urdu, and means "dusty." In the mid-nineteenth century, Tommy Atkin's red uniform jacket was an easy and tempting target on the contested plains of India. In 1846 elements of British cavalry swapped their scarlet for the new camouflage color. It became regulation issue for all troops after the Afghan War of 1878. There was no uniform color at that time; various regiments used berries, coffee, tea, or curry as dyes. By 1900 the British khaki soldier's outfit was standard, even in Europe.

A late nineteenth-century Tommy standing proudly with khaki uniform and early model Enfield rifle.

Author and poet Rudyard Kipling was the renowned exponent of British rule in India. Not only did he immortalize the name "Tommy Atkins" in one poem, but he also recognized the humanity and dignity of a poor servant and thus an entire distant people in the poem "Gunga Din":

"Tho' I've belted you and flayed you,
By the livin' Gawd that made you,
You're a better man than I am, Gunga Din!"

In turn of the century India, the elephant was a good choice for moving heavy field artillery pieces across rugged ground. Luckily for the elephants, they never saw service in Europe.

The Indian army made a substantial contribution to the British war effort by sending 130,000 troops to serve on the Western Front in France and Belgium. In the European context, the Indian forte was cavalry. By 1919 hundreds of thousands Indians had volunteered for service in the war, and nearly eighty thousand died. But it was in theaters other than Europe, especially in the Middle East, that Indian troops were used most effectively.

THE OFFICER

A FORMER PUBLIC SCHOOL BOY,
FINDING HIMSELF AN OFFICER ON
THE WESTERN FRONT, WOULD
STILL BE "PLAYING THE GAME."
IN OTHER WORDS, THE ELITE
VALUES OF OBEDIENCE,
DISCIPLINE, SELF-CONFIDENCE,
AND DEVOTION TO THE TEAM WERE
KEY TO FORMING THE CHARACTER
OF A SUCCESSFUL OFFICER.

FOXHUNTING MEN

Early on, only society's elite could aspire
to be an army officer. And many a son
of a foxhunting family did join the colors,
hoping for a fashionable regiment or an
interesting posting. These young officers
were distinctly proud (or arrogant) of
being gentlemen, and enjoyed all its
advantages and prerogatives.

Above: Officers' sleeve rank in order:
Colonel, Lieutenant Colonel, Major
Captain, Lieutenant, Second Lieutenant

Though officers provided their own uniforms from approved tailors, as a notable author wrote, a shirt and tie of not just the right shade was cause for much comment in the officer's mess. And friendliness with "other ranks" or ordinary soldiers was unthinkable. To be on a first-name basis was against the rules, and would result in a reprimand. That was a social crime only the untutored, such as an Australian or American, might commit.

On the other hand, most officers in WWI were excellent. They were kind, generous, and brave, and did command the respect of their troops.

There were 15,000 army officers in 1914 and more than ten times that four years later. A sizable number of new officers, middle-class and professional men with no previous military inclinations, received temporary commissions. Thrust into the privileged world of army tradition, these men were in essence temporary gentlemen (TG). They were expected to absorb something of upper-class ways, but might be snubbed from above and resented from below. Even so, they were good soldiers. But the TG was sometimes adrift in society, especially when the war ended and his transitory social status evaporated.

An officer from the landed gentry would surely be a riding man, and probably a foxhunting man. In France the officer's personal mount was often the best way to move around on crowded and muddy roads. Caring for the horse was a job for the officer's personal servant or batman.

GOING IN

WHEN AT LAST MOVING INTO
FRONTLINE TRENCHES, TOMMY
CREATED HIS OWN WORDS
AND PHRASES TO HELP TAKE
OWNERSHIP OF HIS GRIM
SURROUNDINGS.

THE FIRING LINE

There were three lines of trenches.
First came the front or firing line, next
the support trench, and then several
hundred yards to the rear was the
reserve trench. Troops would spend a

Often filled with mud and filthy water,
reeking with the smell of decay and
infested with rats, the trenches of WWI
were as dismal as they were dangerous.
But Tommy had a job to do, and moving
through a nighttime maze of trenches,
he did the necessary and disorienting
task of removing the previous occupants.

few days at each location, then out of the trenches altogether for refit, rest, and medical attention. However, when action was hot, a battalion might spend weeks up front. And troops sent to the rear were always on call for labor details, and, if needed, combat.

The wonder is that so many survived.

GRUBBER AND SAP

Soldiers carried entrenching tools, small shovels known as **grubbers**. Using these tools, usually at night, Tommy might begin work on a new trench. If the enemy was nearby, this could be tough and dangerous work. A safer, more roundabout method was to start at either end and work inward. This was called **sapping**. In wet areas, walls of sandbags and timbers prevented collapse of the trenches. And most of northern France and Flanders was wet. Again, the safety of nighttime was cover for work (fatigue) parties who fixed the unstable trench walls.

Trench design zigged and zagged every few feet. The intent was to confine the damage from an exploding shell. A blast would only demolish one section of the trench. Only a handful of men would die in the blast. The next section, protected by an angled wall of earth and sandbags, would be safe.

ROUTINE

A DAY IN THE TRENCHES WAS
EXHAUSTING, WITH MUCH DIGGING,
FILLING SANDBAGS, AND HAULING
SUPPLIES TO BE DONE.

Troops were subject to both concentrated and random shelling. Building sturdy dugouts and shelters became a priority. Heavy timbers, corrugated iron sheets, sandbags, and barrels full of earth were used as reinforcements. Some entrenchments might also have loopholes for rifle fire, although this would eventually draw the fire of enemy snipers.

THE MORNING HATE

For Tommy, the day begins at night. Germans might attack at sunset, so troops man the fire step. The situation is dangerous and sentries look hard into the gathering darkness. Later some troops may sleep, curled in tiny scrapings in the trench walls. Others may talk or play cards for a while.

Still others do the nightly routine of maintenance and repair. Before dawn the fire step is manned once again. The order **five rounds rapid** is given, and rifles quickly shoot at the German line. This is the **Mad Minute**, or **Morning Hate**, an attempt to maintain a martial spirit in still-groggy soldiers. And the German side does exactly the same. After the order to stand down, a tot of rum is issued along with breakfast. Rifles are cleaned and an officer inspects the unit. Then there are more daily maintenance chores.

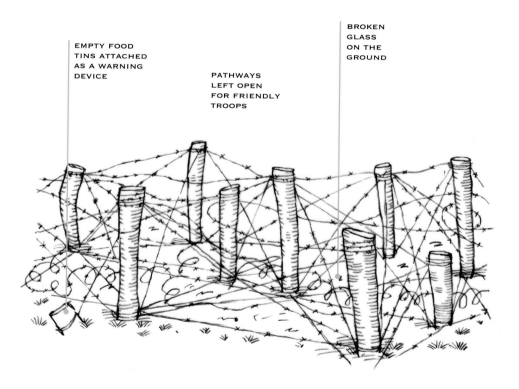

EMPTY FOOD TINS ATTACHED AS A WARNING DEVICE

PATHWAYS LEFT OPEN FOR FRIENDLY TROOPS

BROKEN GLASS ON THE GROUND

Row after row of barbed wire entanglements protected the trenches. An army manual suggested the thickest wire should be closest to the enemy. Wire should be painted or otherwise dulled, and dangling fishhooks added if available. Wooden posts were preferred to metal, since friendly fire would penetrate the wood and not ricochet. However, metal posts could be silently screwed into the ground, not pounded.

FUNK HOLE

FUNK IS AN OLD ENGLISH WORD MEANING "COWERING FEAR." IN THE WAR THE FUNK HOLE WAS SOMETHING LIKE A VERTICAL FOXHOLE.

IN THE TRENCHES

Trench warfare was an affliction, like the plague. With filth everywhere, cleanliness was impossible, though a man was expected to shave daily. There was never enough time for sleep, and the wet climate meant flooded trenches, wet feet, and the possibility of losing toes as a result of trench foot. This malady was so common that soldiers were paired, one looking after the health of the other's feet. The army tried to feed soldiers well, but getting fresh vegetables into Tommy's diet was not easy, and well-being suffered. And food carriers on their way to the front were prime targets for enemy snipers, as were men on their way to latrines.

Each season had its own travails, winter being the worst. Soldiers were issued goatskin jackets, and the "gorblimy" cap with earflaps, but the war years were some of the coldest on record. There was crowding, loneliness, and intense discomfort of every type. There was anxiety over the next order to go into battle, and boredom for those long periods with nothing to do. There was distress, fear, and death when the enemy shelled Tommy's trench. More and more this particular brand of warfare

seemed a humiliating, and maniacal sort of torture. And yet Tommy endured, sometimes cheerfully, sometimes not. Tommy had his pride, and discipline, and loyalty to his mates in the trench. And he endured by dreaming of the next letter from home, and the day he would be rotated out of the front line.

TALKING TRENCH

Funk Hole: one-man shelter scraped out of the side of a trench.

Elephant Dugout: large dugout.

Cubbyhole: same as funk hole.

Bivvy: a temporary shelter, bivouac.

Gasper: a cheap cigarette.

Woodbine: brand of cheap cigarettes.

Crummy: itchy from insect bites.

Coot: the ever-present louse.

Fed-Up: originated in the Boer War, where it's meaning today originated.

Kultur: so-called superior German civilization, especially its rigid and brutal military aspect; grimly humorous.

THE HINDENBURG LINE

The German army was prepared to stay in the occupied lands of France and Flanders. They dug in and built an impressive series of fortifications and concrete bunkers. The comforts in their underground burrows, called the Hindenburg Line, were something the Allies couldn't aspire to match. The resilient German shelters were so well constructed that even now some remain, nearly intact. For the British and French military planners, their entrenchments were merely temporary, and would be abandoned as they pushed the enemy back, and moved onward.

Despite the official specifications for trench construction, in practice sometimes a trench was hardly more than a few connected shell holes. This particular example was described as a secondary trench. The trenches that connected the first, second and third lines were known as communication trenches.

EVERYTHING TRENCH

ON THE WESTERN FRONT TRENCHES WERE SO EXTENSIVE THEY CREATED THEIR OWN ECOSYSTEM, INCLUDING NEW DISEASES, NEWSPAPERS, AND WORKS OF ART.

TRENCH RATS

The rat was a constant and extremely unwelcome worry. It feasted on the remnants of food scraps, and what was especially ghastly, the unburied dead in no-man's-land. Since the rats were bold, and said to be big as cats, feline conscripts were not effective. A terrier on the other hand might make quick work of a local infestation. Men organized rat hunts wielding club and bayonets; firearms, though, were usually prohibited in the crowded conditions. The only thing that was sure to rid the trenches of rats was an enemy gas attack.

TRENCH NEPHRITIS

Trenches were unsanitary in almost every way imaginable. The local earth, long fertilized with animal manure, could easily cause infection in a minor wound. It was also a breeding ground for disease. Trench Nephritis, or inflamed kidneys, affected thousands of troops. The specific cause is not clear but might be related to hantavirus, carried by mice.

TRENCH FEVER

This condition with symptoms of high fever, headache, dizziness, and muscle complaints could strike quickly and incapacitate for weeks, and it was recurring. In 1915 British doctors recognized this common complaint as a new disease. The conditions needed for the spread of trench fever were exhaustion and related impaired immune system, both ordinary in front-line troops. Body lice-carrying microbes were the actual cause of the disease. It was impossible to eliminate the lice entirely, but new sanitation procedures helped reduce infections.

TRENCH FOOT

This was yet another disease caused by the dreadful living conditions at the front. In was not unusual for troops to stand in the muddy trenches, in foul puddles of water, for hours if not days at a time. Keeping feet, socks, and shoes clean and dry was difficult. In these conditions feet became cold and numb, with blood flow impaired, and feet could turn gangrenous rather quickly. The condition was similar to frostbite, without frost. Prompt treatment was needed, but still men lost toes and even feet. The condition was so common that it was a cause for disciplinary action. One solution was to team men up, to attend to one another's foot care.

Trench Mouth: yet another disease brought on by stress and deprivation; bleeding gums and foul breath were symptoms.

Trench Frogs: on occasion a plague of croaking frogs would descend on the waterlogged trenches; walking in trenches filled with squirming creatures was unnerving.

Trench Cats: cats in substantial numbers went to war, as mousers and mascots; they were also used to locate poison gas, in what must have been a suicide mission.

Trench Journals: official news was censored and scant, and so many British outfits published their own newspapers; much of the content was humorous or irreverent; the most famous was "The Wipers Times," named after Ypres, the place and the battle.

A Canadian song from 1917 sums up a fighting man's feeling about trench life:

There's a little wet home in the trench,
    that the rain storms continually
    drench.
A dead cow close by,
    with her hooves in the sky.
And she gives off a beautiful stench.
Underneath us, in place of a floor
Is a mess of cold mud and some
    straw,
And Jack Johnsons roar as they
    speed through the air,
O'er my little wet home in the trench.

TRENCH ART

The individual instinct to create beauty was not altogether lost in the war. Bored soldiers, and even more bored prisoners of war, created art from the available mounds of military detritus. Most objects were decorative, and the most common were made from discarded brass shell casings. They were engraved, illustrated, and otherwise fashioned into striking vase-like items. Many pieces were done in the then current Arts and Crafts style. Almost all trench art is anonymous, and much must come from after the Armistice, as with the wooden cigarette box shown above. Though most often thought of as soldier's folkart, the degree of finish indicates that local craftsmen had created some things for the souvenir trade. And later a few commercial companies churned out trench art style objects.

THE KING'S SHILLING

COCKNEY SLANG, LOCAL BRITISH DIALECT, AND OLD-TIME ARMY JARGON ALL CONTRIBUTED TO THE BRITISH TOMMY'S COLORFUL WWI SONGS AND RHYMES.

Hush, Here Comes a Whizz-Bang

Hush, here comes a whizz-bang.
Hush, here comes a whizz-bang
Now you soldiermen get down
*   those stairs*
Down in your dugouts and say your
*   prayers.*
Hush, here comes
a whizz-bang,
And it's making right
for you.
And you'll see all the
wonders of
*   No-Man's-Land,*
If a whizz-bang hits you.

A new recruit was said to be "taking the King's shilling," and as the phrase continued, he would then be required to "do the King's bidding." In 1914 the lowly British private was actually paid one shilling per day. And he was also given a bonus of twenty-four pounds on signing, from which he had to pay for his own uniform.

Previously Tommy was perceived as being at the bottom of the social heap. With the war going, press and public perception charged. Now he was working-class, and an upright fellow. Though cheeky, with cockney irreverence, he was ever the staunch supporter of King and Country.

The words of marching songs, and other rhymes, accurately followed Tommy's changing moods. Often the infantry's own words were attached to well-known melodies, hymns, or music hall ditties.

Fred Karno's Army

(Fred Karno was a popular entertainer)

We are Fred Karno's army, the ragtime
*   infantry.*
We cannot fight, we cannot shoot,
*   what bleedin' use are we?*
*   And when we get to Berlin*
*   we'll hear the Kaiser*
*   say, 'Hoch, hoch!*
*   Mein Gott, what a*
*   bloody rotten lot,*
*   are the ragtime*
*   infantry.'*

Kaiser Bill

*Old Kaiser Bill
went up the hill
To see the terrible
    slaughter,
He fell down
And broke his crown,
And so he bloody well
    oughter.*

Why Did We Join

*Why did we join
    the army, boys?
Why did we join
    the army?
Why did we come to
    France to fight?
We must have been
    bloody well barmy.*

If You Want the Old Battalion

*If you want to find the old battalion,
I know where they are,
I know where they are,
I know where they are,
If you want the old battalion, I know
    where they are,
They're hanging on the old barbed wire,
I've seen them,
I've seen them,
Hanging on the old barbed wire.*

Saki's Song

*While shepherds watched their flocks
    by night
All seated on the ground,
A high-explosive shell came down
And mutton rained around them*

Saki was the writer H. H. Munro,
who was killed in the trenches.
His last words were "put out that
damned cigarette."

SMELLY AND BARKER

SINCE DEADLY WEAPONS WERE
TOMMY'S CONSTANT COMPANIONS,
IT SEEMED RIGHT TO DOMESTICATE
THESE OBJECTS WITH FRIENDLY OR
HOMEY NAMES, OR NAMES FROM
AROUND THE BRITISH EMPIRE.

Many new weapons were developed in the war, but from 1914 to 1918 the British infantryman depended on the Enfield, Vickers, and the Webley. Certainly there were a few variations, and a bit of subtlety, but there were few hardware innovations for the Poor Bloody Infantry.

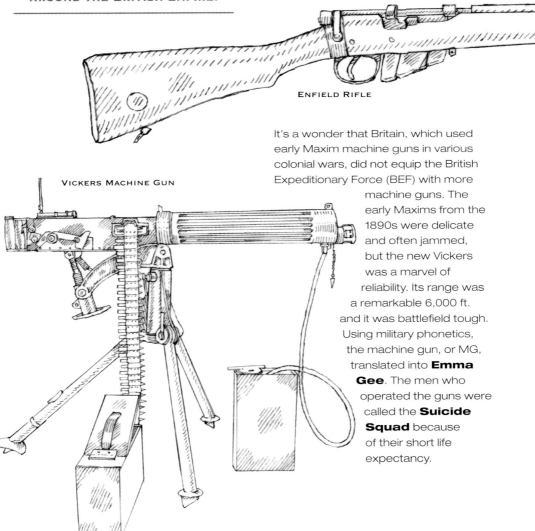

ENFIELD RIFLE

VICKERS MACHINE GUN

It's a wonder that Britain, which used early Maxim machine guns in various colonial wars, did not equip the British Expeditionary Force (BEF) with more machine guns. The early Maxims from the 1890s were delicate and often jammed, but the new Vickers was a marvel of reliability. Its range was a remarkable 6,000 ft. and it was battlefield tough. Using military phonetics, the machine gun, or MG, translated into **Emma Gee**. The men who operated the guns were called the **Suicide Squad** because of their short life expectancy.

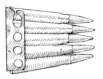

The .303 bullet was slightly off-balance, so when it hit a target, it spun and could do tremendous damage.

Tommy was thought of primarily as a spear-carrier, a man from the Middle Ages engaged in siege warfare. Once past no-man's-land and into the enemy trench, who could resist the bellowing and lunging Tommy with his fixed bayonet?

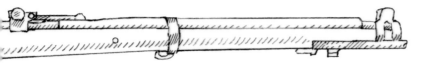

SMELLY

The Lee-Enfield rifle was an advanced weapon with tremendous firepower. It had speed of operation and a large magazine, and it was rugged, perhaps the perfect battlefield rifle. It made the riflemen of the BEF the fine marksmen they were. It was short, and handy, almost like a carbine. Even a novice can identify the Enfield with its blunt front end. Its official name was "Short, Magazine, Lee-Enfield" or SMLE Mk III, hence the nickname **smelly**.

BARKER

The Webley was hefty. With bullets it weighed nearly four pounds, and it was big. The .455 bullet was a man-stopper, and for close combat it was accurate for self-defense. As well as officers, tank-men, machine gunners, and pilots carried the Webley. It wasn't a toy, and officers with only a Webley were known to capture enemy bunkers. Nineteenth-century dueling pistols were called **barking irons**, and this modern revolver kept the name.

Today attaching a cord, or lanyard, to a pistol may seem odd. But this is a practice that originated in the cavalry, when an unexpected bump could mean a lost pistol. And this became a tradition with officers throughout the army. Officers didn't carry rifles. They were leaders, not fighters, but they carried a pistol for personal protection. And in a battle officers were busy. They brandished a walking stick to wave men on, and then for signals they held a whistle. A lanyard on a Webley kept it safe and ready.

THE WEBLEY

THE BIG PUSH

Seldom have high spirits, careful planning, and incredible bravery been dashed to the ground so cruelly. On July 1, 1916, during a massive assault on the German trenches at the Somme River, the attacking British forces were beaten.

Above: A BL-8 howitzer was the sort of heavy gun used at the Somme. It was in service from 1915 until the end of the war. The basic idea of the howitzer, with its high shell trajectory, was that it could target enemy positions even located behind a hill.

Left: For many years, along with the mustache, the walking stick had been a symbol of authority. No matter how young, the chap with the cane always seemed mature enough to be in charge.

Left: Soldiers needed a reliable and quick way to tell time. And so the wristwatch, previously a woman's fashion accessory, became a must-have item for the trenches. The metal guard protecting the watch face was a useful feature of the service watch. Sometimes also called the wristlet, the name wristwatch didn't catch on for some time.

THE SOMME

July 1, 1916. The new British army, recruited in 1914, and now trained and outfitted, was ready for the Big Push. One hundred thousand men were ready to advance on German lines at the Somme River, taking pressure off the French still engaged at Verdun. Armored tanks, a British secret weapon, were there; also there were huge flame-spurting weapons to engulf enemy trenches. There was a heavy barrage and troops went over the top at 7:30 a.m. Immediately everything went tragically wrong. The big British guns had not done their job, and tanks broke down. British troops emerging from their trenches were mowed down. Twenty thousand died in one day. It was the worst day ever for the British army.

Below: Flares illuminated the nighttime battlefield, and were also used as signals. The best-known flare gun was the compact Very pistol, which shot flares called Very lights. Like the machine gun and barbed wire, it was American, invented by Lt. Very for saving lives during disasters at sea.

TRENCH LADDERS

Tommy might justifiably become nervous when he saw scaling ladders brought forward into the first line trench. The order to go over the top would surely be coming soon. One of the many misfortunes during the attack of July 1st, or Z Day, was that troops just emerged from the trench were immediately hit by German fire, and toppled backwards onto the still-occupied scaling ladders below.

In more successful attacks, scaling ladders might be carried along over no-man's-land. They would be thrown over tangles of enemy barbed wire, making a clear path for the attacking troops.

OVER THE TOP

SCRAMBLING OUT OF THE TRENCHES, BRITISH TROOPS ATTACKED THE ENEMY, AGAIN AND AGAIN, OFTEN SUFFERING HORRENDOUS LOSSES.

This was Tommy's ultimate moment. He was trained to fight, but sustained by loving thoughts of home and loyalty to his unit.

Eventually new tactics were tried and Tommy had a better chance of surviving no-man's-land. Closer coordination between artillery and infantry was key. The best-remembered and most honored victory using this tactic was the Canadian assault on Vimy Ridge in April 1917.

The Canadians climbed the slope to the Ridge, during a snowstorm, and in hand-to-hand fighting drove back the deeply entrenched enemy. It was the British slang for an impending attack or battle, a **Grand Slam**. The one hundred thousand-man Canadian army was a major contribution to Britain's fighting strength. And they, as well as the Australians, were thought of as Britain's shock troops.

Left: This drawing is based on a memorial statue in Victoria, British Columbia.

OVER THE TOP

(from *Over the Top* by Arthur Guy Empey)

"We crouched around the base of the ladders waiting for the word to go over. I was sick and faint, and was puffing away at an unlighted fag. Then came the word, 'Three minutes to go; upon the lifting of the barrage and on the blast of the whistles, " 'Over the Top with the Best o' Luck and Give them Hell.' " The famous phrase of the Western Front. The Jonah phrase of the Western Front.

"I glanced again at my wrist-watch. It was a minute to four. I could see the hand move to the twelve, then a dead silence. It hurt. Everyone looked up to see what had happened, but not for long. Sharp whistle blasts rang out along the trench, and with a cheer the men scrambled up the ladders. The bullets were cracking overhead, and occasionally a machine gun would rip and tear the top of the sand bag parapet. How I got up that ladder I will never know. The first ten feet out in front was agony. Then we passed through the lanes in our barbed wire. I knew I was running, but could feel no motion below the waist. Patches on the ground seemed to float to the rear as if I were on a treadmill and scenery was rushing past me. The Germans had put a barrage of shrapnel across No Man's Land, and you could hear the pieces slap the ground about you."

THE ROLLING BARRAGE

The British by 1917 had devised the **rolling barrage**. This was a slowly moving curtain of artillery fire, which just barely preceded the troops as they crossed no-man's-land. The barrage prevented the emergence of German troops from their deep dugouts until it was too late, and the British troops were already upon them. This and better ways of locating and destroying enemy guns made a difference. However, each battle was unique. At the tragic Battle of Passchendaele in late 1917, oceans of mud made artillery movement difficult, and the fired shells sometimes sunk into the mud without exploding.

TALKING TRENCH

Wave: a line of men who go over-the-top in an attack; there are usually several waves.

Windy: to be nervous or apprehensive…as in before an attack.

Ricco: a ricocheted bullet

Rum: distributed every morning; especially welcome while waiting for zero hour.

Parapet: the trench top that Tommy must go over.

Mud: the all-pervasive environmental feature of northern France and Belgium.

In Front: to be in no-man's-land.

Dud: an unexploded shell; during the Somme dud shell rates were as high as 30%.

TRENCH FIGHTING

AFTER CROSSING NO-MAN'S-LAND
TOMMY NEEDED HIS WITS, AS
WELL AS HIS RIFLE WITH FIXED
BAYONET, TO SUBDUE THE ENEMY.
THOUGH DISCIPLINE AND TRAINING
WERE VITAL, IN PRACTICE A FIGHT
IN THE TRENCHES WAS A
FREE-FOR-ALL.

Techniques for subduing the enemy in their trenches depended heavily on close coordination between specialized troops.

These text excerpts are from *Knowledge for War: Every Officer's Handbook for the Front*, by Captain B. C. Lake, published in 1916.

Storming the Trench

"In taking a line of trenches, it is essential to remember that the attack will take place on a relatively small front, by a large number of men, and therefore when the trenches are finally reached there will be great over-crowding in them. To extend along them as quickly as possible is of paramount importance; otherwise the casualties in these crowded areas will be exceedingly heavy. This important work is usually the duty of the grenadier party, which, in the attack, should be in the rear of the front line of infantry.

In exceptional cases they may be employed in advance of, or with, the assaulting lines. By creeping forward within throwing distance of enemy trenches they can cover bayonet assault with a shower of grenades.

Immediately on reaching the trenches the grenadier-party should start bombing those still occupied by the enemy, so that they may be cleared, and the crowded troops be able to extend along them.

Regarding the formation of grenadier storming parties. The objective is to gain possession of as much as possible of enemy's trench. In a narrow trench the only portion of an attacking party coming into contact with the enemy is the head.

Method of Advance

Rapidity of movement is essential. Crawling and stalking gives the waiting enemy an advantage. The leading bayonet men move along the trench, from corner to corner, in a succession of rushes, followed by first grenadier and carrier. Grenadiers throw as directed by bayonet men. The duty of the leading bayonet men is to protect the grenadiers at all costs.

The second grenadier and second carrier follow the leader, keeping one corner behind. If the first grenadier is put out of action the carrier takes his place till next grenadier comes up.

Each party is to be regarded as reserve to the party in front. Each party must carry coloured flags (or some substitute agreed upon) to mark its position in captured trenches. On reaching objective, flags should be placed in such a position as to be easily seen by supporting troops. The code of colours must be changed for each attack.

As more bombs are required they must be passed up from the rear, and replaced from the established depots."

"Training for the final assault: The use of the rifle butt at close quarters. The butt can be used with effect against an opponent's jaw or in the region of the heart. Also to be considered are the various methods of tripping, and the use of the knee."

ATTACK

IT SEEMED THE BRITISH BULLDOG MASCOT WAS THE INSPIRATION FOR THE NEW BATTLE TACTIC OF "BITE AND HOLD." VICTORY WAS ELUSIVE, BUT IT WAS POSSIBLE TO NIP AWAY AT THE ENEMY. THIS WAS FIGHTING THE WAR BIT BY BIT. PERHAPS VICTORY WOULD COME BY 1920 OR 1921.

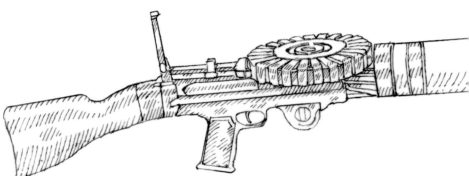

It is unclear exactly who called the Lewis light machine gun the **Belgian Rattlesnake**, but it was a good name for this efficient weapon. Its American inventor first built the gun in Belgium, although the war soon caused Col. Lewis to move to Britain. There, Birmingham Small Arms Company (BSA) built the gun. It was far lighter than the unwieldy Vickers, it had a similar rate of fire, and with fewer parts it was generally trouble-free. In combat the Lewis gun, like any other machine gun, was a prime target. However, being highly mobile, the Lewis gun crew could move often to escape enemy spotters.

The armies of Britain and France, versus Germany, were too evenly matched for victory by either side. Experience showed that dug-in defenders could almost always fight off an attack. New types of weapons, such as poison gas or flamethrowers, didn't upset the stalemate, and only added to the ongoing slaughter. And soon enough these innovations were copied by the other side. In theory the British tank should have ended trench warfare. But even when tanks achieved an actual break-through, as at Cambrai in 1917, the situation was hazy, and communications were bad. Reinforcements were not called for, and the enemy plugged the hole in their line.

THE LEWIS GUN

As of the year 1917, a foolproof method for breaking through enemy lines had not yet been discovered. Clearly an attack by row upon row of men, à la the Napoleonic Wars, did not work and only led to mass casualties. But new tactics and increased use of the Lewis light machine gun were beginning to give Tommy a much-needed boost in firepower. Firing a Lewis gun, advancing British platoons

matter of kill or be killed. A grenade party consisted of nine men, grenade throwers, grenade carriers, and bayonet-wielding riflemen. When the men were close enough, shrapnel grenades were lobbed into an enemy trench. Bayonet men then entered to dispatch any survivors. The squad would then move on to the next section of the trench, while preparing for the inevitable enemy counterattack. Major Ainslie, the man who wrote the 1917 textbook on the subject, said, "The importance of grenade work cannot be over- estimated and one can imagine numberless cases when a grenade is more useful than any other weapon."

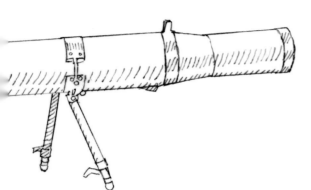

forced German defenders to stay under cover. When close enough, another section of troops with bags of deadly grenades (called Mills bombs) would unload on the enemy trench. This was a tactic that worked, and the Germans learned to hate the Lewis Gunners. It's said a captured British soldier with an embroidered LG on his cuff was subject to immediate execution by vengeful Germans.

GRENADES

The task of a bombing party, attack an enemy trench with a shower of grenades, was highly dangerous. Once on a raid in enemy territory, it was a

STUFF

IT WAS THE BIG GUNS, AND
THEIR POWERFUL SHELLS, THAT
DROVE THE TROOPS FROM THE
BATTLEFIELDS AND INTO THE
TRENCHES. TOMMY'S WORD FOR
THE STORM OF FLYING STEEL
WAS SIMPLY "STUFF."

"ARE WE DOWNHEARTED?"

Before a battle, millions of artillery shells, barrage and counter-barrage might be exchanged. The destruction was immense, but the protection given by a well-constructed trench was remarkably good. However, even in a quiet sector an unexpected random shell could demolish a trench, and kill, perhaps even vaporize, some unlucky troops.

Tommy's best defense was irony, and a dark humor that deflated the power of the big guns. Contemporary writers called this attitude "cheerfulness"; even so the effect of artillery on morale is obvious. The following are excerpts from selected quotes attributed to Tommy from early in the war:

"The object of the great proportion of artillery the Germans employ is to beat down the resistance of their enemy by a concentrated and prolonged fire, and to shatter their nerve with high explosives before the infantry attack is launched."

"The artillery is what harasses the men most. They soon developed contempt for German rifle fire, and it became a very persistent joke in the trenches. But nearly all agree that German artillery is 'hell let loose.' "

"A corporal in the Motor Cycle Section of the Royal Engineers writes: 'At first the German artillery was rotten. Three batteries bombarded an entrenched British battalion for two hours and only seven men were killed.' "

"Writing home is certainly done under circumstances which are apt to have a disturbing effect upon the literary style. 'Excuse this scrawl,' writes one soldier, 'the German shells have interrupted me six times already, and I had to dash out with my bayonet before I was able to finish it off.' "

"There are immense shells filled with high explosives which detonate with terrific violence and form craters large enough to act as graves for five horses. The German howitzer shells are 8 to 9 inches in caliber, and on impact they send up columns of greasy black smoke. On account of this they are irreverently dubbed 'Coal-boxes,' 'Black Marias,' or 'Jack Johnsons' by the soldiers."

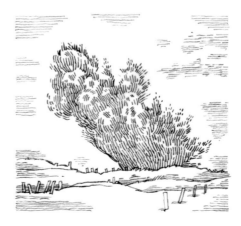

"What a Frenchman describes as the 'new British battle-cry' is another source of amusement. Whenever artillery or rifle fire sweeps over their trenches some facetious Tommy is sure to shout, 'Are we downhearted?' and is met with a resounding 'No!' and laughter all along the line."

Euphemism was a weapon at which the British Tommy excelled. Giving each category of enemy artillery shell a homespun name was a way to domesticate the legitimate dread they all experienced.

The Whizz-Bang was attributed to the noise made by shells from German 77mm field guns. The name was derived from the fact that shells fired from light or field artillery traveled faster than the speed of sound.

The Nonstop was an enemy shell that has passed well overhead.

The Jack Johnson was a German howitzer shell 8 to 9 inches in caliber, and on impact it sent up columns of greasy black smoke.

The Silent Susan was a high velocity shell.

Moaning Minnie referred to the German trench mortar or *Minenwerfer*, the term carrying overtones of familiarity and humor.

ENGLISH, ANYONE?

SNIPERS, MACHINE GUN BULLETS, SHELL EXPLOSIONS, AND A MULTITUDE OF OTHER DANGERS WERE ALWAYS WAITING FOR THE UNWARY OR UNLUCKY.

Here is another nonsense sentence similar to examples shown earlier: "Then I grabbed a packet from an emma gee, did a belly-flop, and waited for a hot cross bun on a night roll."

TRANSLATION

Grab a packet was one of the many slang phrases for being hit by enemy fire. **Emma Gee** is the army phonetic signalese (or phonetic alphabet) for MG, meaning machine gun. A **belly flop** was falling to the ground quickly during an enemy attack, or when hit.

Ambulances prominently displayed the Red Cross symbol, hence the term **hot cross bun**. A **night roll** describes an ambulance out on a nighttime mission.

Right:
A German machine gun team

EMMA GEE

BELLY FLOP

BODY SNATCHER

Stretcher bearers worked long, and hard, especially after a battle, when there was a multitude of wounded and dead to retrieve. The job could take one or two days, and it was dangerous, since random enemy shells might still be falling. This was strenuous work due to muddy conditions, when one stretcher might require four or even six men to carry. The first destination for the wounded man would be the Regimental Aid Station located in the reserve trench line. Early in the war, band members were used to carry stretchers, but there were high losses, and to preserve the bands, others were given the job. The name **body snatchers** did triple-duty: it was a Tommy on a night raid, a sniper, and also a stretcher bearer.

TWO BUSES

MUNDANE AND DEPENDABLE, BATTLING BUSES WERE FOUND THROUGHOUT FRANCE. THOUGH ONE "BUS" WAS MERELY AN AFFECTIONATE FIGURE OF SPEECH.

For generations of delighted Londoners, one still-operating WWI bus called 'Ole Bill, after the famous cartoon character, appeared in Remembrance Day parades.

Surprisingly, after the war, hundreds of buses returned to England, and provided additional years of service on the streets on London.

LONDON TRANSPORT

Imagine a peacetime Tommy waiting for a London bus in early 1914. Just six months later he may have found himself waiting for the exact same bus on a muddy road in France. Of course now that bus was painted khaki, and had become official army transportation.

The bus itself would have been the relatively new B-type. The War Office had requisitioned more than one thousand, and when they reached France were

still red and covered by all their old advertising placards.

Columns of buses were used to transport large numbers of BEF troops and cargo. Just weeks after the war began, even the London bus drivers, now in khaki, were also shipped to France.

The buses were robust and served throughout the war, occasionally in unusual roles. Some were converted to rolling anti-aircraft platforms, and others were used as mobile coops for messenger pigeons. They survived to the end. In 1919 buses entered Germany carrying the British army of occupation.

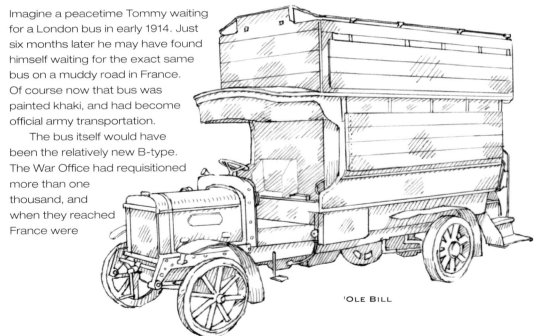

'OLE BILL

Below: The Bristol F.2, active from 1916 onward, did it all. It was a fighter, observation plane, and light bomber, plus a ground attack aircraft. This rugged aircraft was in service, especially in the Middle East, until at least 1932. It was called the "Brisfit" and also the even more muscular sounding "Biff."

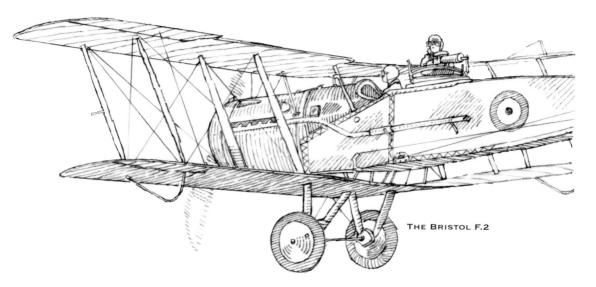

THE BRISTOL F.2

THE OLD BUS

The army's talent for slang and euphemism included the unique language of the Royal Flying Corps (RFC). A new pilot on the Western Front in 1917 had an estimated life span of six weeks. Calling his aircraft a "bus" surely added much-needed comfort and humor to an uncertain situation.

While not all British airplanes in WWI had official diminutives, all the famous Sopwith fighter airplanes had them:

Sopwith Tabloid, 1914
Sopwith Baby, 1915
Sopwith Strutter, 1916
Sopwith Pup, 1916
Sopwith Camel, 1917
Sopwith Snipe, 1918

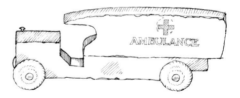

Above: Even a 1920s wooden toy ambulance, simple though it is, has the authentic proportions and essential look of WWI vehicles. The name "old crate" seems appropriate for their boxy appearance. The term is doubly appropriate, since vehicles left the factory packed in huge wooden crates.

Two More Buses

Far from being an interesting sideshow, aircraft were essential to trench warfare, both as an observer, and also as a combatant.

Gun Bus

From nearly the beginning, the accuracy of the big guns was vastly aided by the ever-present observation aircraft. Remove the planes, and the accuracy of enemy artillery would be diminished. Hence the introduction of the fighter plane, with the job of clearing the friendly skies of enemy intruders. Some of the early fighter planes were slow pusher planes, which meant they had the engine in the back, and gun aggressively in the front. German fighters were better, so the RFC losses were very high. Early fighter planes were the Vickers F.B.5, known as the Gun Bus, and the similar F.E.8, or **Fee**, shown here.

Strafe

"*Gott strafe England,*" or "God punish England", was a German phrase often scrawled on the walls of captured French villages, **strafe** meaning punish. From the German viewpoint, no country deserved punishment more than Britain, apparently for all its alleged crimes throughout history.

Soon Tommy picked up "strafe" as a description for all forms of punishing enemy fire, be it artillery, rifle, or machine gun. Eventually, though, "strafe" came to mean machine guns raking ground troops from the air. And this became more common as sturdier airplanes, sometimes with heavy armor, emerged. As well as the trenches, strafing planes could reach targets like railroad and ammunition depots, far behind the lines. Both sides did it, and the best RAF strafing planes were the Brisfit, SE5a, and especially the Sopwith Camel.

Right: The old British pushers did valuable work, but the French had better planes, and many RFC squadrons used various types of the excellent Nieuport scouts.

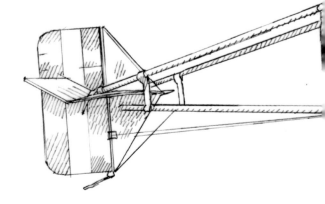

Above: The British SE5a was a good fighter aircraft, and it was used for strafing attacks. However, when flying low, its radiator-cooled engine was easily damaged by enemy ground fire. The Sopwith Camel had a massive air-cooled rotary engine that could absorb more punishment.

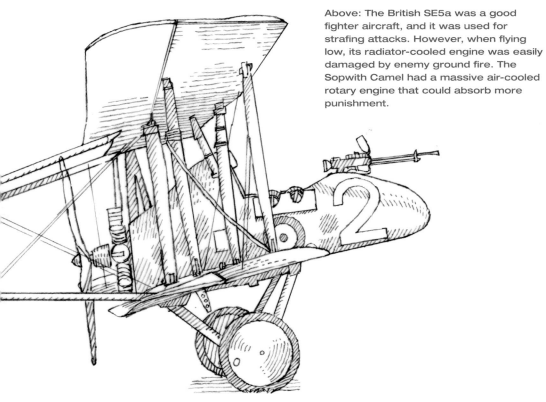

MACONOCHIE

IN THE TRENCHES TOMMY ATE BREAD AND BULLY BEEF, HE DINED ON EGGS AND CHIPS IN INFORMAL RESTAURANTS BEHIND THE LINES, AND IN QUIET SECTORS HE GREW HIS OWN VEGETABLES IN LITTLE GARDENS.

DINING AL FRESCO

London newspaper readers were told of the sumptuous al fresco meals front-line troops enjoyed. To paraphrase one supposed letter…"What magnificent food we have, and there is so much of it. Just think, tomatoes and bacon for breakfast every day." Such accounts were mostly wishful thinking. Of course the army wanted to feed the troops, but the enemy wasn't cooperating. Field kitchens were knocked out by artillery. Hot food and water, carried in large backpack-like containers called **dixies**, were special targets for German snipers. The term was "death by dixie." The safest way to have a cuppa tea on the firing line was to heat some water with a candle.

With all these dangers and difficulties, the British soldier had to be considered well-off. He was supposed to receive 4,000 calories a day, and most often he did. On the other hand, provisions for the German soldier were meager, with an emphasis on large amounts of potatoes. But over the years, Tommy also began to feel the pinch. German U-boats were devastating shipments of food from Canada, the U.S., and Argentina. The 1914 allocation of 10 oz. of meat per day for a soldier had by 1916 been reduced to 6 oz.

TALKING TRENCH

Shackles: soup or stew made from leftovers.

Baby's Head: meat pudding.

Spotted Dog: currant pudding.

Gippo: juice or gravy.

Pozzy: jam.

Axle Grease: butter.

All troops were happy to get food packages from home, but it was customary for officers of means to regularly purchase hampers of delicacies and fine wine, from London's upper-crust department stores.

TOMMY'S MV

With resupply impossible, soldiers in the trenches relied on the bags (usually empty sandbags) of simple provisions they carried. There would be bread, hard biscuits, 12 oz. tins of bully (corned) beef, tinned jam, tinned butter, pork and beans, and packets of cigarettes. It was probably just a notch above mere sustenance, and each article of food brought complaints from hungry Tommies.

The Huntley and Palmer biscuits were said to be hard enough to break teeth, and they had to be soaked in water to make them edible. After eating salty **bully beef**, troops were parched. Water was in short supply and sometimes tasted of gasoline from contaminated carrying cans. So in the middle of rain-soaked, muddy trenches, thirst was a constant problem. And least of all, the jam was so invariably apple/plum, that even London readers of *Punch* magazine knew of the Tommy joke about the frequency of apple/plum jam being served.

The most famous tinned food of them all was Maconochie, a thin stew with a little meat, and a few slices of turnips, and potatoes. According to the army it was Tommy's MV, meat and vegetables. Upon opening a cold tin, a clotted fatty substance was seen to have risen to the top. One Tommy compared the cold concoction to "garbage when eaten." But when heated apparently it was not too bad, and some soldiers liked it.

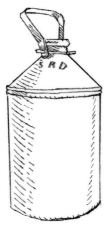

Right: A tot of rum was normally issued in the morning to warm the soul, and help withstand the horrors of war. The gallon size stoneware jug was large enough for sixty-four men. Stamped into the jug were the initials **S.R.D.**, meaning Service Ration Depot. But to Tommy the letters meant "Soon Runs Dry" or "Seldom Reaches Destination."

Above: Tommy Cookers were small personal food heaters using blocks of a solid fuel called Kampite. The device was advertised as "safe for use in dug-outs, tents, and trenches." It was just right for heating Maconochie, if you had the time. But first the contents had to be placed in a mess tin, or the Maconochie tin might explode.

For It

The British Army was known for being strict but fair, with the emphasis on strict. Even the enemy agreed on this point, as one German general claimed, "Germany would have won the war with such discipline."

One problem for military justice was to assign punishment that did not deplete troop strength. A soldier sent to prison was evading service at the front. But prison wasn't easy, guards were not sympathetic, days were long, and everything was done at double-time. Arthur Guy Empey, an American who joined the British army, wrote:

> "In the British Army discipline is very strict, one has to be careful to stay on the narrow path of government virtue. There are about seven million ways of breaking the King's Regulations; to keep one you have to break another."

But generally the British soldier was compliant, and found the army's rules and regulations tolerable.

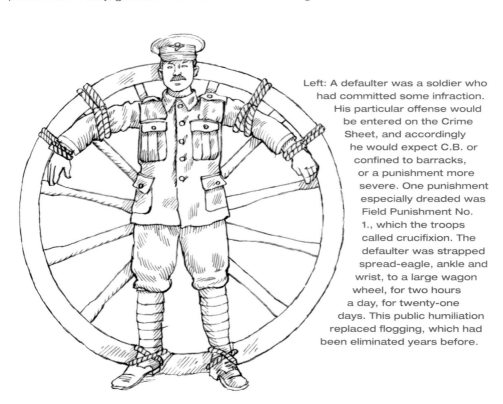

Left: A defaulter was a soldier who had committed some infraction. His particular offense would be entered on the Crime Sheet, and accordingly he would expect C.B. or confined to barracks, or a punishment more severe. One punishment especially dreaded was Field Punishment No. 1., which the troops called crucifixion. The defaulter was strapped spread-eagle, ankle and wrist, to a large wagon wheel, for two hours a day, for twenty-one days. This public humiliation replaced flogging, which had been eliminated years before.

WINDY

"Windy" was trench vernacular for the nervous soldier. However, seldom did a windy soldier abscond. When it came to deserting, the trick was to get away with it. Leaving a dark trench in the dead of night was one way to illegally depart from the war. With luck it might be possible to get totally clear of every trace of the British army, but the deserter's problems were just beginning. Being in the heart of France, not speaking the language, with no food, and still in uniform would probably mean a quick capture. Most deserters were caught within two weeks. And the deserter was unlikely to get any help from the local French population. Most likely, they'd alert the authorities. Riding on a train would require papers. French and British military police were looking for spies, stragglers, and deserters.

Getting on a ferry to England would also be impossible without a military pass.

Another tactic for slipping away was used by some formerly convalescent soldiers, returning from Britain, and again on their way to the front. It was to simply get lost in the crowds at the docks. Of course, was there a plan after that?

Desertion was a most serious crime, comparable to mutiny, and punishable by firing squad. Not only was desertion an insult to military order, it was nothing less than a sign of cowardice, an especially powerful word in a time when personal honor was the highest virtue. Very few serious offenders were actually executed, but the threat was always there.

As one general said, "If you abolish the death penalty you might as well abolish the army."

GONE WEST

DEATH IN WARTIME IS ALWAYS UGLY, BUT DOUBLY SO IN WWI. THE FIRST IMPRESSION NEW TROOPS HAD WHEN APPROACHING THE FRONT WAS THE OVERPOWERING SMELL OF DECAY.

CENTENNIAL YEAR

In the WWI Centennial Year of 2014, a total of 888,264 red poppies surrounded the Tower of London, one poppy for each British or colonial soldier killed in the Great War. Out of all of Britain's fighting men, 17% of the officers, and 12% of other ranks were killed, or died in some other manner. The great killer was artillery. Up to 80% fell victim to the big guns. But like most WWI statistics, all numbers were questionable.

GONE WEST

When death came to the trenches during a relative quiet time, the soldier who had "clicked it" was put on a stretcher, removed from the trenches, and carried to an advanced first aid post. This was the same procedure used for a seriously wounded Tommy. During all this movement away from the front lines, the dead soldier was in fact, geographically speaking, going west, hence the probable origin of the common euphemism for death.

At some point personal effects would be placed in a packet for eventual return to next of kin. And the family was promptly informed. A short but dignified burial, with chaplain and trench-mate pallbearers, took place behind the lines at the regimental cemetery. The remains were sewn in a blanket and lowered into the grave. A small sealed glass bottle with a slip of paper containing information about the deceased was also buried, as a sort of miniature time capsule.

TALKING TRENCH

Snuffed It: killed, as a candle is snuffed.

Clicked It: killed.

Thrown a Seven: killed; bad luck, mate.

On the Wire: killed, as in the song "Hanging on the Old Barbed Wire."

Landowner: dead and buried.

Rest Camp: a cemetery.

Stiff's Paddock: burial ground.

Sgt. Harry Cator, VC

Right: More than a million 5 inch round memorial plaques were issued to next of kin. It looked like a large coin, and was known as the "Dead Man's Penny."

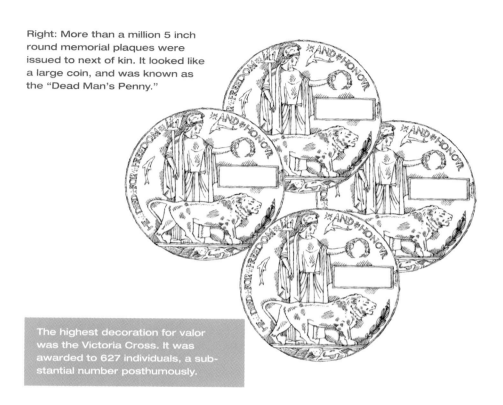

The highest decoration for valor was the Victoria Cross. It was awarded to 627 individuals, a substantial number posthumously.

Cpl. Thomas Bryan, VC

Pt. W.J. Milne, VC Posthumous

NEURASTHENIA

STRAIN, EXHAUSTION, CONSTANT SHELLING, AND ALL THE ACCUMULATED HORRORS OF WAR CAUSED AN EPIDEMIC OF PSYCHOLOGICAL BREAKDOWNS OF EVERY TYPE.

MO

Charlie Adolphus Sampson joined the British army when he was thirty-three years of age, during the patriotic excitement of 1914.

He was a fortunate man and survived four and a half years of war. Previously a Harley Street doctor, Sampson had a quiet sense of adventure (he was the first doctor in South London to drive an automobile), as well as a sense of duty. Coming from a long line of Royal Navy officers, after joining he soon asked the army for a transfer to the navy, but apparently the War Office needed his services in the Royal Medical Corps. Sampson served in France as a Medical Officer (MO) with a rank of Captain Surgeon.

Family hearsay has it that when he first returned home in 1918 not only would he never speak of what he had experienced, but he was also so "shell shocked" for a short while he couldn't physically speak at all.

Actually, because he was an officer, the medical diagnosis would have been the vague term "neurasthenia." It was the lower ranks with the same symptoms who were said to be shell shocked. This was a medical condition that had many causes, but it was simply the endless chaos, noise, and horror that caused the human mind to shut down. Victims of shell shock might tremble, cry, or exhibit the "thousand mile stare," which was looking at some distant point but seeing nothing.

Though there were various treatments for this mental condition, the best was loving care, and the comforts of family life. After the symptoms had passed, Dr. Sampson resumed his practice, but now specialized in medical hypnosis, one of the wartime treatments for shell shock.

Dr. Sampson had been cured of the war. As the years passed he bought an ex-lifeboat and sailed with his family whenever he could. He wrote and published several books of sailing stories. He painted watercolors, and invented and patented several safety gadgets for sailors. He went to the theater, and played piano. By any standards, Dr. Sampson lived a full life.

In 1940 when Charles Sampson died, his son, also a doctor, was far away on a British warship, in the midst of World War II.

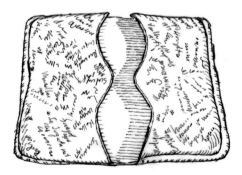

Above: A relic of Capt. Sampson's wartime service is this leather cigarette case. All over the case, written in a tiny script in brown ink, are the various locations, on the Western Front and others, where Sampson was active in the Great War.

A Surgeon in Arms, by Captain R. J. Manion, M.C., Canadian Army Medical Corps, 1918:

The Common Soldier

You occasionally meet what the English call a rotter, but his kind is exceedingly scarce. After all, the finest type is the ordinary common soldier, without any special qualifications, who, day in and day out, night in and night out, performs the dirty, rough, hard, monotonous, and often very dangerous, tasks of the Tommy; who does his duty, grumbling perhaps, swearing often, but does it without cowardice, without hope of honor or emolument, except the honor of doing his duty and doing it like a man. When his work is done he comes back, if still alive and well, to sleep in wet clothes, on a mud floor, under a leaky roof or no roof, often hungry, or his appetite satisfied by bully beef and biscuit.

Yes; with all his swearing, despite any lead-swinging, the finest type of all, the real hero of the war, is the ordinary common soldier!

"Doughboy trench talk consisted of British slang, mangled French words, and hobo and cowboy vernacular."

CHAPTER FOUR

AMERICA
WITH THE DOUGHBOY

THE DOUGHBOY

JOURNALISTS IN BOTH AMERICA AND FRANCE WERE LOOKING FOR A NICKNAME FOR THE AMERICAN SOLDIER: SOMETHING LIKE THE BRITISH TOMMY. FIRST CHOICE WAS "SAMMY," A NAME THAT WAS HEARTILY DESPISED BY EVERY AMERICAN SOLDIER. ANYTHING ELSE WOULD BE BETTER, EVEN DOUGHBOY.

THE LIBERTY HELMET

The army experimented quite a bit before adopting the Model 17, which was the American version of the British Brodie helmet. Dr. Bashford Dean, curator of arms at New York's Metropolitan Museum of Art, came into the army as a major and was tasked with creating a brand-new American helmet. His designs, called the Liberty Helmet, were based on fifteenth-century Italian armor. Thousands of prototypes were quickly produced and field-tested in France, but they were heavy and looked much like the German steel helmet. All in all, the British helmet, while not perfect, was a better choice; plus, the British had 400,000 helmets available for incoming American troops.

During the six months of hard fighting, from June to November, the enlisted man in the American Expeditionary Forces (A. E. F.) received on the average:

- Slicker and overcoat, every 5 months.
- Blanket, flannel shirt, and breeches, every 2 months.
- Coat, every 79 days.
- Shoes and puttees, every 51 days.
- Drawers and undershirt, every 34 days.
- Woolen socks, every 23 days.

Above: The Montana Hat
Introduced in 1911, the campaign hat with its broad brim and rain-deflecting peak was a favorite with American troops. However, it proved too bulky for trench warfare. Also, the hat was made from rabbit-fur felt, mostly from Argentina, and the rabbit population couldn't keep up with demand.

Above: The American M 1917 was better than the British original in several subtle ways. Most importantly, it was made from a better grade of steel, giving the wearer more protection.

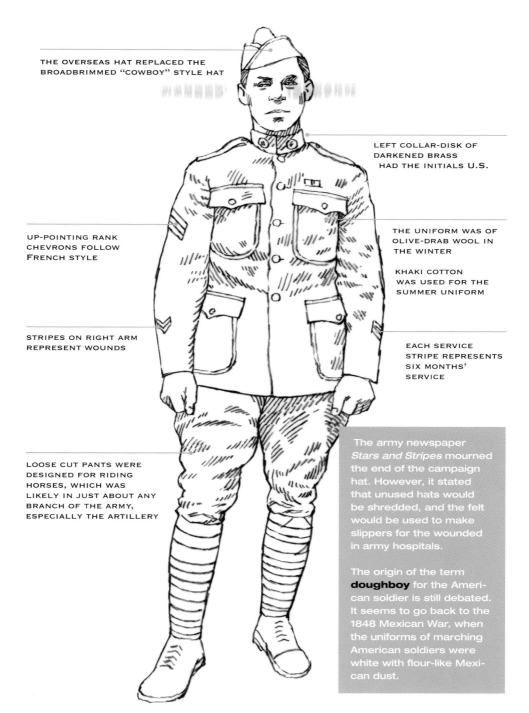

THE OVERSEAS HAT REPLACED THE
BROADBRIMMED "COWBOY" STYLE HAT

LEFT COLLAR-DISK OF
DARKENED BRASS
HAD THE INITIALS U.S.

UP-POINTING RANK
CHEVRONS FOLLOW
FRENCH STYLE

THE UNIFORM WAS OF
OLIVE-DRAB WOOL IN
THE WINTER

KHAKI COTTON
WAS USED FOR THE
SUMMER UNIFORM

STRIPES ON RIGHT ARM
REPRESENT WOUNDS

EACH SERVICE
STRIPE REPRESENTS
SIX MONTHS'
SERVICE

LOOSE CUT PANTS WERE
DESIGNED FOR RIDING
HORSES, WHICH WAS
LIKELY IN JUST ABOUT ANY
BRANCH OF THE ARMY,
ESPECIALLY THE ARTILLERY

The army newspaper
Stars and Stripes mourned
the end of the campaign
hat. However, it stated
that unused hats would
be shredded, and the felt
would be used to make
slippers for the wounded
in army hospitals.

The origin of the term
doughboy for the American soldier is still debated.
It seems to go back to the
1848 Mexican War, when
the uniforms of marching
American soldiers were
white with flour-like Mexican dust.

THE A.E.F.

THE AMERICAN EXPEDITIONARY FORCE WAS A HUMAN TIDAL WAVE. BY WAR'S END IN 1918, IT CONSISTED OF AT LEAST TWO MILLION MEN, WITH MORE ON THE WAY. IT ALSO INCLUDED A FLOOD OF UP-TO-DATE AMERICAN EQUIPMENT OF EVERY SORT.

DEVIL DOGS

A relatively small contingent of Marines was sent to Europe. The Marines were well trained, and motivated, and had experienced officers. For years they had been on the cutting edge of America's small wars in Latin America and the Pacific. Two of the early American battles were hard-won Marine victories in June of 1918. In the spring of that year, Germans broke through Allied defenses, and were again close to Paris. The Marines entered the battle at Belleau Wood and Château Thierry, and after hard fighting with serious losses, helped stop the German advance.

The story goes that the German troops were so impressed by the Marines, fierce fighting ability that they gave them the name "**Devil Dogs**."

GRAVEL AGITATORS

The U.S. army consisted of the small Regular Army and National Guard, plus the mass of drafted men, new to military life. These men had received a short six months of training at camps in the United States, and continued with advanced training after arriving in France. A preferred method of building discipline and endurance were long, often exhausting marches. However, the brutally cold winter of 1917/1918 was a painful time to learn soldiering.

From *Stars and Stripes*, Feb. 1918:

> "Every moment on the treacherous ice was as perilous as learning to skate. In the first five hundred yards there was not a man in the regiment, except the mounted officers, who escaped a tumble, and lots of them went down again and again."

Despite the ice, "gravel agitators" still seemed a good name for soldiers on a march.

OVERTHERE

ONCE IN FRANCE, U.S. DOUGHBOYS
WERE GIVEN TWO MORE MONTHS
OF TRAINING. THEN THEY SPENT
AN ADDITIONAL MONTH IN A QUIET
SECTOR OF THE FRONT. DURING
THAT TRAINING, FRENCH LIAISON
OFFICERS KEPT CLOSE TABS
ON THE PROGRESS OF THE
AMERICAN TROOPS.

A close relationship between France and the U.S. was vital. But there were disagreements and dueling national egos. The French wanted to command all American armies, but U.S. General John J. Pershing insisted that Americans should command their own troops. Eventually Pershing won.

Of thirty-four American divisions, twenty-eight trained next to the French before taking up their own frontline positions.

Experienced French liaison officers helped untried and overeager Americans adapt to battlefield situation with various practical suggestions, such as, in battle, keep casualties down by using ground cover while advancing toward the enemy. And keep proper spacing between the American rolling artillery barrage and the attacking doughboys who followed. They advised ways to avoid ambushes and other tactical dangers, and proposed techniques for unsnarling massive traffic jams that often bogged down American convoys. And French weapons were available to the not-yet fully equipped Americans, including 75mm field artillery, the French Chauchat automatic rifle, and Nieuport and SPAD fighter planes.

Here a French officer watches American artillerymen loading gun caissons at a railway depot for transportation to a battle area.

WAR DIARY

ORDERS SAID, "NO DIARIES. THEY MAY CONTAIN IMPORTANT MILITARY INFORMATION, AND COULD BE CAPTURED BY THE ENEMY." NOT EVERYONE FOLLOWED ORDERS, HOWEVER, AND MANY COMPELLING STORIES HAVE TURNED UP IN DIARIES THAT HAVE BEEN DISCOVERED. SGT. NATHANIEL ROUSE'S SPARSE WORDS IN HIS 1918 ENTRIES DESCRIBE THE DOUGHBOY'S ROUTINE.

Jan. 11 Rained. Came back from drill early. Had lecture. Some got packages. I did not. Drilled afternoon.

Jan. 25 Foggy day. Drilled all day. Worked out a little battle. F Co. gave a little entertainment. Got steel helmets. Bed 10:00.

Jan. 27 Cloudy and foggy. Got my hair cut. Band concert, played the SS Banner. Got 10 letters; Dell, Ma, and Lillie. Red letter day.

Feb. 6 Clear. The Germans sank the "Tuscania." I suppose lots of mail went down.

Feb. 9 Clear, warmer. Went out with full equipment to fight the 166 Ohio Inf. Didn't get back until 6:00pm. Played poker (even).

Feb. 14 Clear. Went out all day with packs, came back 6:30. Got payed. Got my hair cut off to an inch off my head.

Feb. 21 Clear. Walked all over the town the Germans occupied for 21 days. Got a room, some room. Nothing could prepare the troops for the reality of war

Mar. 4 Snow. We opened fire about 11:30 am, and believe me it was some noise.

Mar. 5 Arrested [?] in quarters. Left camp NY at 3:00am. Arrived at front line trenches. Under fire for first time.

Mar. 6 Clear. Some day. On an outpost 5/8 of a mile from the Boche. The Boche put over a gas cloud and some shell fire.

Mar. 7 I don't feel like writing. E Co. lost 23 men and one officer. They were caught in a dug out by a big shell. [He mentions his life was saved on this day because of a "switch," and this transfer saved his life.] A shave in the morning; a foot-wash at night—every day.

Mar. 11 Left the trenches at 8:30 for camp NY. After arriving had some meal. Letters from Dell. I wish she could explain things.

Mar. 16 Very beautiful days now. Got up at 6:00 to go on wood detail. Came back and went to bed.

Mar. 18 Beautiful day. Went out to cut wood again, good exercise. Got box from Dell. Had a little party.

Mar. 26 Snow, sunshine, rain. Got paid, it sure did look small this time. Had supper in a French house.

Mar. 30 Rainy. Didn't do anything but drill a few hours. It was a soft snap.

Apr. 4 Clear in morning & rainy in evening. Went out to range did not make a hit. Went to movies at YM.

The 1918 battles of the Meuse-Argonne were a terrible introduction to war. It was less painful to remember those months as merely an exercise for toy soldiers.

Apr. 15 Rain. Had a lecture in morn. Had our gas masques on for an hour. It was horrible. I hope they get us out of here soon.

Apr. 19 Cloudy. Drilled all day. Had gas masques on for an hour. A year ago today I enlisted.

Apr. 26 Cloudy. We don't drill anymore. Too close to the Boche lines. Worked on dug out all day.

May 8 Clear. I was on guard for 3 hours. (Gas) Hung around the YM. Capt. Kelly came back.

May 9 Clear. I can't sleep nights with the scabies. Guess I will see the doc tomorrow. Lannon came back.

May 10 Beautiful day. Went to the hospital today for scabies. Had a ride all the way in YM trucks.

July 15 Oh God, what a night. They shelled us something terrible. I had my gas masque on for 4 hours straight.

July 16 The Germans came over after the shelling. The French retreated and left us in charge.

July 17 Quiet night. We held them and they started in again, about 6 in morning, to come over.

July 18 I was in hell for 6 hours. We held them back. I haven't had any sleep or anything to eat for 50 hours. I don't know how I stand it.

Aug. 1 We had to fall back. We were within 200 yards of them. Had no artillery to back us.

Aug. 2 We have two platoons left. I am afraid I will be next. God how lucky I was.

Aug. 3 The Boche have fell back 10K. We have to establish contact with them. We have them again.

Aug. 4 Our 3rd battalion lost 350 men. I tell you I feel blue. I don't think I will ever go home. All the old bunch are gone.

Slumgullion

Slumgullion was an old-fashioned meat stew, and it was a specialty of WWI army field kitchens. Sometimes in the trenches, "slum" just didn't make for fine dining. Arriving cold and late, sometimes it was just bearable, like life in the trenches.

Redefinitions

These two pages might be considered a slumgullion, a little bit of everything, in the hope of giving some of the flavor of the doughboy's life. The words presented below are not new, but in the context of the 1918 German Spring Offensive, and the American pushback, they took on new shades of meaning.

Through the Mill

This originally meant working in a hot and dangerous steel mill. Now when an army unit was pulled out of the front line, and had 30% losses, it was obvious the men had been through the mill.

In WWI America had the standing Regular Army, the National Guard, and the new draftee-heavy National Army. The bronze collar disk shown is Regular Army.

Replacements

After training together for months, an outfit became a family. Then after a deadly time at the front, for those who survived, arriving replacements seemed like strangers entering the family. And for the arriving replacements, they were entering the domain of the cautious old-timers.

Looking Their Best

In the trenches the bottoms of long overcoats were soon weighed down by a thick coat of mud. French seamstresses were hired to shorten the coats for a fee of one franc each. For another franc, barbers gave a haircut, with hair trimmed close on the sides, to discourage lice.

Prohibition

Other armies had their wines and spirits, but not the U.S. army. And on January 1919 a constitutional amendment forbidding the sale of alcoholic drink in the United States was approved. A prime advocate had been the Women's Christian Temperance Union. Soldiers feared the WCTU's efforts to also ban cigarette smoking in the trenches.

The Y.M.

Soldiers had a love-hate feeling toward the Y.M.C.A. In France there were 4,000 huts and tents dispensing much-needed comfort, entertainment, and a taste of home. The only problem was that the Y.M. man behind the counter was fit, healthy, and perfect army material. But instead he wore an officer's uniform, had preferred housing, and didn't fight. Eventually the Y.M.C.A. changed its rules and only accepted men above draft age.

Wig-wag is the flag waving cross-field signal system first used in the Civil War. It was still taught in WWI, despite the more advanced field telephone, and later the radio.

The sea of mud in northern France could sidetrack any motor vehicle. Only mules and men could navigate the terrain. Mules are both intelligent and affectionate, and are especially fond of mare horses. So in a mule convoy, a mare with bell attached to its harness was placed in lead position. This "bell mare" would lead the docile mule teams.

Mule handlers were know by the fearsome name of **muleskinners**, and their rough language was not fit for man nor beast, and actually it just made the mules more stubborn. Hoping for more efficiency, the army ordered an end to such rough talk. Muleskinners should no longer speak in harsh "United States" (as American English was sometimes called) to their charges.

Stars and Stripes was the official army newspaper in France, published between Feb. 1918 and June 1919. Though official, it was honest but not stuffy. The staff consisted of enlisted men with newspaper backgrounds. After the war, some went on to found the *New Yorker* magazine. Browsing through the Library of Congress website, which has a complete collection of the paper, one can find material on how Americans perceived the war, along with a showcase of the great examples of American journalism. One short item seemed humorous in 1918, but is less so in today's world.

"The war will soon be over. An Ohio man will end it. He has suggested to U.S. Marine Corps officials in Washington that they direct their aviators to drop potato bugs over Germany. He declares there are no potato bugs in the kaiser's realm, and since the 'spud' is absolutely essential to Germany's economic welfare, the dropping of 'Murphy destroyers' over the Rhine country would quickly terminate hostilities. Simple, isn't it? Marine Corps officials think so."

And a joke:
"Well, Bill, how are you getting along with your French?"
"Fine! I know the words for wood, straw, beefsteak, and suds; what more do I want to get by with?"

In the Trenches

The trench closest to the enemy was the fire trench. It was lightly occupied except in attack or defense. Parallel and behind that was the support trench, which was the strongest point of defense.

Trenches were constantly punished by weather and enemy shellfire. To keep the trench walls intact, lengths of timber, wicker mats, sheet iron, and dirt sods were used. Though sandbags were the most common building material, the cloth was liable to rot in just a few weeks.

All communication, fire, and support trenches, etc., were named. At the entrance of trenches were guideposts with directions to various locations. Without these signs, the network of trenches was a bewildering maze.

COMPANY

Some of the dugouts were used for advanced first-aid dressing stations. Dugouts with shell-proof covers and bomb stores were built into especially strong points to avoid damage from shell blasts.

SOME BASIC RULES

- no smoking or talking at night

- every man was to wear his equipment, except backpack

- always be attentive to foot care, especially sentries standing on wet ground for hours

and an officer must…

- see that his men were properly fed

- know what every man was doing at all times

The connecting communication trenches, some of them over a mile in length, might run back into roads or villages.

BLOTTO

BLOTTO, BOZO, AND BUSTED... DOUGHBOY TRENCH TALK OFTEN CONSISTED OF BORROWED BRITISH SLANG, MANGLED FRENCH WORDS, AND OLD-TIME HOBO AND COWBOY VERNACULAR. HOWEVER, AUTHENTIC AMERICAN SLANG WORDS WERE CONSTANTLY BORN OR REPURPOSED.

DOUGHBOY TRENCH TALK

According to author and literary critic H. L. Menken, much doughboy slang was transplanted from its original U.S. setting.

Busted: in WWI, now meant to be demoted. What it meant previously is unclear.

Outfit: This was a cowboy word borrowed for war use. Any group of men, from a platoon to an army, might qualify for the word outfit. Today it's a word for any organized group.

Hardboiled: a term that implies a person no longer has the soft, squishy insides of a civilian, and that conventional morality counts for nothing. This term seems likely to have come from the fighting doughboys in France. The hardboiled movies of the 1930s, featuring ruthless gangsters with their smoking tommy guns, were direct descendants.

Blotto: totally drunk, to the point of unconsciousness.

Bozo: a stupid, inept, rude person, or clown; probably an early vaudeville character. Several WWI American journals use the word bozo to describe totally oblivious personnel.

Buddy: a comrade or valued friend. Some soldiers believed the term came from New York City, where it was thought everyone was called buddy.

Cherched: (from *chercher*, meaning to chase), getting some needed piece of equipment, or any other thing. It is comparable to scrounge, or some would call it borrowing while neglecting to obtain permission.

Conked Out: refers to an airplane engine stopping mid-flight. The word is said to reproduce the last sounds of the failing engine...conk-conk-conk, until it conks out completely.

Dogs: feet. After an exhausting march a soldier or Marine might say, "my dogs are barking."

Doughgirl: the female version of doughboy, but applied to the young women of the Red Cross, who were well known for passing out doughnuts.

Frog: a derisive name for the French. It could be used as a prefix to apply to anything relating to France, such as frog dame, frogland, and frogtown. This is an old British term, going as far back as the Middle Ages.

Gadget: a catch-all term for any newfangled contraption or thing, but mostly referring to a mechanical device, usually of a puzzling nature.

Gold-Fish: canned salmon.

The Great War: as WWI was known to the doughboys in the trenches, as well as most other people.

Hop-Over: a short-duration raid into enemy territory.

Jake: meaning everything is fine, or cool…no problem, man. It was first used in 1914 and might be a corruption of the French "chic." Again a popular 1930s tough-guy word.

Kaput: from the German, meaning finished or done. A dead German would be kaput.

Knock Koo-Koo: to knock out, knock unconscious, or kill.

Pushing up Daisies: to be killed and buried in France.

Land Battleship: an early name for British army tanks. In 1903 H. G. Wells prophesized tanks in his story "The Land Ironclads."

Lid: a steel helmet.

Pass: to die.

Punk: bread, as it was called in prewar New York City breadlines.

Roughneck: artilleryman.

Shellitis: experiencing the horror of war, and its devastation and human toll, first hand; an initial first step toward eventual shell shock.

There were tough-guy phrases that came into their own during the war.

"Tell it to the Marines," meaning only the brave men of the Corps were capable of dealing with a dicey situation; a choice rejoin-der in street-talk of the post- war decades.

"I'll say so," "I'll tell the world," and **"You said it"** were emphatic variations on the simple word "yes."

Trench Tips

WORDS OF WISDOM FROM ARTHUR GUY EMPEY, AN AMERICAN VOLUNTEER IN THE BRITISH ARMY, WHO WENT ON TO WRITE TWO HIT BOOKS OF ADVICE FOR DOUGHBOYS AND THEIR FAMILIES.

ENTRENCHMENT TOOL

"When an infantryman reaches France he quickly learns that in trench fighting "the shovel is mightier than the rifle." With his entrenching tool, the infantryman can lay out a ditch or series of trenches, build a road, rebuild a village, construct a dugout, or dig an artillery emplacement."

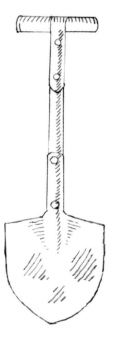

HANDY SANDBAGS

"Before going over in an attack, strap two or three empty sandbags on your equipment. Later on these may prove invaluable. If you get in a hot corner where you are exposed to rifle or machine-gun fire, it is an easy matter to fill these sandbags with earth, thus making a cover that will prove effective against bullets.

Sandbags also make excellent covers for the feet while sleeping. Just put your feet in a couple of sandbags and you will be surprised to learn how warm they keep. And, spread over with straw, sandbags make comfortable beds."

THE RICOCHET

"Never throw rubbish, the remains of your rations, or tin cans out in front of your trench. This is liable to cause bullet ricochets; the rations will not only feed rats, but after decaying will often cause disease. Remember it is a court-martial offense to do this."

Tea-time

"When water is scarce, the weather cold, hot water unobtainable, and there is no time to heat any for shaving—use tea. This may be a trifle sticky, but it is a fact that tea has a softening influence on the most bristling and copper wire whiskers."

Mud

"Mud is a great protection from shells. While crossing a muddy field or open space, if you hear a shell which is going to burst in your vicinity, drop down flat in the mud—the chances are a hundred to one that you will not be hit. The shell buries itself very deep in the mud and explodes, the mud preventing the fragments from scattering to any great extent."

Curiosity

"When the soldier enters the fire, or frontline trench, he is generally very curious and wants to poke his nose into everything. He has a great desire to look 'over the top' of the parapet and get a glimpse of the German lines. Restrain this curiosity, because it is liable to result in serious injury to yourself. You must remember the Germans have a wonderfully efficient system of sniping, and are always waiting for someone to expose himself."

Wet Shoes

"To dry wet shoes, heat small pebbles and place them in the shoes. Be careful not to have the pebbles hot enough to scorch or crack the leather."

Traffic Control

"In nearly all sectors of the Western Front communication trenches are about three feet wide and are used as one-way streets. These one-way streets prevent confusion in the relief of battalions in trenches. One communication trench is used for the entrance of troops, and the other for the departure of troops."

KEEPING VALUABLES:
A GOOD WAY TO KEEP PAPERS, TOBACCO, MATCHES, OR A HANDKERCHIEF DRY IN RAINY WEATHER WHILE IN THE FIRE TRENCH IS TO SEW A LITTLE POCKET ON THE INSIDE OF YOUR STEEL HELMET LARGE ENOUGH TO CARRY THESE ARTICLES.

ORDERS

REMOVED FROM THE COMPARATIVE FREEDOM OF CIVILIAN LIFE, THE NEW SOLDIER ENCOUNTERED ARMY RULES FOR JUST ABOUT EVERYTHING.

THE PULL-THROUGH

Rifles must be kept clean (using a piece of cloth called a **pull-through**) and in good condition while in the trenches. They will be cleaned every morning during an hour appointed by the company commander for that purpose. Platoon commanders will be responsible that section commanders superintend this work. All rifles except those used by sentries are to be kept in racks during the day.

AUTO-TRUCKS TO THE FRONT

Transportation, by auto-trucks and wagons, is utilized to a point as near the lines as possible, to carry the packs of the men, the auto rifles, extra ammunition and other heavy equipment. When the distance is great the men themselves should be carried by auto-truck; this saves time and fatigue. The men will carry rifles loaded and locked, full cartridge belts, gas masks, and all other lighter equipment.

BLACK JACK COFFEE

There are but two cooking utensils, the tin cup and the frying pan. After the bacon is fried and rice made in the tin cup, the cup is washed out and the man is then ready to fry his potato and boil his coffee. The cup is filled two-thirds full of water and the coffee placed in it and boiled until the desired strength is attained. To prevent the coffee from boiling over, a canteen of water should be handy and water thrown in whenever the coffee begins to boil over. When the coffee is strong enough, the addition of cold water will settle the grounds, and **Black Jack Coffee** will result. In the meantime, cut the potatoes very thin and fry them in the bacon grease and the meal is ready.

A Dry Rub

Cleanliness of person, clothing, and bedding should become a habit of life with the soldier; but some men will always require watching and admonition. These habits are: personal cleanliness; regulation of diet; avoidance of excesses; wearing suitable clothing; keeping the bodily processes at work (kidneys, bowels, and skin); taking sufficient exercise, preferably in the open air; rest of body and mind, with recreation for the latter; maintaining the surroundings in which one lives in a cleanly state. Bathing is easily the most important requirement in matters of personal hygiene; men should bathe as often as conditions of life in barracks and camp will permit. On the march a vigorous **dry rub** with a coarse towel will often prove an excellent substitute when water is not available.

A Tonic

Because there is a constant battle with the elements, there must be continual care for drainage, support structure, sanitation, and storage. Repairs must be made due to the effects of bombardment. New work must be carried out for better security, communication, and observation. The work done in the open usually consists of repair or rearrangement of wire entanglements, digging new listening posts, etc. Fighting patrols, composed like reconnaissance patrols, guard workers, but their best protection is in silence and concealment. This work, like all operations conducted outside the protection of the trenches, offers a valuable **tonic** to the morale.

The men will be formally inspected twice daily. Particular attention will be paid to the health of the men, including the condition of their feet and their clothing. Each man must have at least one pair of dry socks always available. Arms, gas masks, and other equipments will also be rigidly inspected.

HEROES ALL

AMERICANS OF EVERY TYPE PERFORMED COUNTLESS ACTS OF BRAVERY IN THE WAR. MOST REMEMBERED ARE SGT. YORK, AND FLYING ACE EDDIE RICHENBACKER, BUT THE LIST OF AMERICAN HEROES IS SEEMINGLY ENDLESS. ODDLY ENOUGH, ALSO REMEMBERED ARE A DOG AND A BIRD.

carried stretchers, dispensed words of hope, and gave last rights to the dying. When the Germans were expected to overrun their lines, the commanding officer offered him hand grenades for self-protection. Father Duffy declined, preferring to "stick to his own trade."

JOYCE KILMER

Before the war Joyce Kilmer had been a promising writer. He had written *Trees and Other Poems*, published in 1914. The poem "Trees" eventually became incredibly famous. But it was not only the poem that was noteworthy. There was also the chilling footnote, that the young poet had been killed by a sniper's bullet through the brain on July 30, 1918.

Kilmer had asked for combat duty, and his fearless intelligence-gathering missions inspired devotion from his unit. During his time in France he had also become friendly with Father Duffy, and after Kilmer's death, Duffy gathered Kilmer's notes and included them in the book *Father Duffy's Story With an Historical Appendix by Joyce Kilmer*.

FATHER DUFFY

At the northern end of Times Square, now called Duffy Square, stands a massive bronze statue nearly eight feet tall. It represents Father Francis P. Duffy in full WW1 battle dress. Duffy had been a beloved neighborhood priest who had gone to war as chaplain of New York's own "Fighting 69th" regiment. As chaplain, in the midst of battle he never left the wounded and dying. He

MOM-NEXT-DOOR'S SON

Popular WWI author Arthur Guy Empey gives tribute to America's mothers for supporting the patriotism of their soldier-sons:

> "Mother, feel proud that your son is in the army where he belongs. Do not worry more than necessary over the trials and tribulations that he must endure, but look forward to the time when you and the rest of the community will be lining the curb, greeting him on his victorious return from France."

He goes on:

> "American Mothers, the American soldier, the Stars and Stripes, Uncle Sam, our Country, God's Country, salute you! We are proud to be your sons! We dip our colors to you, and we hope and earnestly pray that you also are proud that we are your sons."

MISS

The name Linnie Leckrone should be better known, since she was an authentic combat hero of WWI. She was a dedicated nurse who joined the Army Nurse Corps in 1916. Her rank was "miss," (Miss Leckrone), as there were no actual military ranks for women. Linnie Leckrone arrived in France and in July 1918 was sent into the fierce battle raging at Château-Thierry. This was the great German drive that was killing hundreds of Americans every day. Her aid post was Gas and Shock Team 134, and it was continually under enemy artillery fire. Her job was to help troops with major wounds, as well as those who had been gassed. She was awarded the Citation Star, which in 1932 became the Silver Star, the third-highest medal for combat valor. Miss Leckrone was never informed, and in 2007 her daughter was presented with the medal.

SERGEANT YORK

Hollywood in 1941 made its selection for All-American soldier hero of WWI in the movie "Sergeant York." York was modest, a man of few words from the American heartland, and peace loving, although when angered there was no stopping him. And he was a crack shot. Plus, Gary Cooper played the role beautifully. Actually, before Alvin York became a man of peace, he had been a hell-raiser in the Tennessee backcountry. And that was useful when he met the Germans in the Meuse-Argonne offensive of October 1918. York's unit ran into several German machine guns and took heavy losses. He crept behind and began picking off the Germans one by one. More Germans appeared, and sharpshooter York continued his "turkey shoot." Out of ammunition, he used his '45 pistol until the German major in charge surrendered his 132 men, and 32 machine guns. For this York won the Medal of Honor.

THE MONK

Monk Eastman was a dangerous character, a brawler, thug, and killer from the gangs of New York's Lower East Side. He was also a strange guy, and his early life is more legend than fact. But clearly he preferred the lowly dive bars to the pet store on Broome Street he used as a front. He sometimes worked as a strongman for New York's corrupt political machine, and though arrested he never was behind prison bars very long—until after an especially bloody street battle in 1903 when he ended up in Sing Sing for ten years. Monk was not your typical doughboy, being a jailbird, with a body covered with scars from bullets and knife fights, being a relatively elderly forty-four years old. But in France he was a fighting terror and a loyal comrade, and he came home a hero. However, he returned to his old life, and in 1920 was shot dead. Remembering better days, his fellow troops arranged a military funeral for him.

THE MESSENGER PIGEON

Today Cher Ami's little grey taxidermied pigeon body stands at attention on a wooden stand in the Smithsonian. Without a doubt a remarkable bird, Cher Ami, a messenger pigeon, had saved the lives of the 197 soldiers who were the survivors of the Lost Battalion. In the confusion of the Meuse-Argonne fighting in September 1918, the 500 man battalion had been surrounded by Germans, and it was also being shelled by American artillery. Two previous pigeons with messages pleading for the artillery to stop were both shot out of the sky. Cheri Ami was their last hope, carrying a message with their location and the plea "for Heaven's sake stop it." Though severely wounded, the pigeon made it back to headquarters, and the barrage was halted. Cher Ami was a national hero, but its wounds had been so bad, including a lost leg, that he died the next year.

STUBBY

Stubby was a mutt with short legs, a wide smile, and the look of a bull terrier. As a pup, he had been smuggled by a doughboy in New Haven, Connecticut, on board a troopship. Eventually he was sent to France with the 102nd division. Stubby was originally a mascot, but he learned the soldier's trade. He could hear incoming shells from a distance, sniff out poison gas, act as a guard, and comfort the wounded. He could even tell the difference between U.S. and German uniforms, or so it was reported. At Château-Thierry he was given a dog uniform that was quickly covered with medals, and at some point was promoted to sergeant. The press turned Stubby into a sensation. He marched in parades and even shook hands with President Wilson. Maybe it was just too much; some veterans complained that one dog was given more honors than two million men.

U.S. Weapons

America had created some of the best small arms in the world. The big problem was to get them to Europe before Germany won the war.

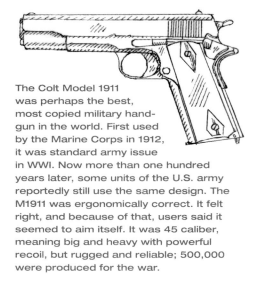

After the Spanish American War, and the following guerrilla war in the Philippines, the army realized it needed a powerful handgun with more stopping power. The master weapons-maker John M. Browning had a winning design. It was a 45 caliber semi-automatic with a seven round magazine. In one test, the pistol fired six thousand rounds, and when the pistol got too hot it was immersed in water to cool it. This was the famous Colt Model 1911.

The Colt Model 1911 was perhaps the best, most copied military handgun in the world. First used by the Marine Corps in 1912, it was standard army issue in WWI. Now more than one hundred years later, some units of the U.S. army reportedly still use the same design. The M1911 was ergonomically correct. It felt right, and because of that, users said it seemed to aim itself. It was 45 caliber, meaning big and heavy with powerful recoil, but rugged and reliable; 500,000 were produced for the war.

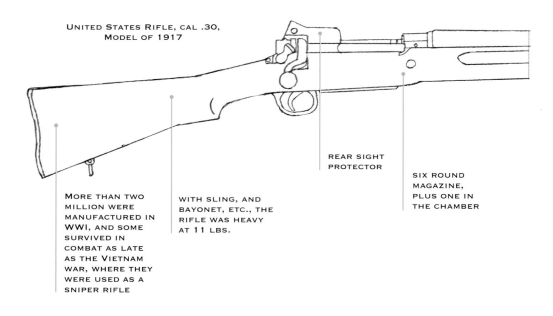

UNITED STATES RIFLE, CAL .30, MODEL OF 1917

MORE THAN TWO MILLION WERE MANUFACTURED IN WWI, AND SOME SURVIVED IN COMBAT AS LATE AS THE VIETNAM WAR, WHERE THEY WERE USED AS A SNIPER RIFLE

WITH SLING, AND BAYONET, ETC., THE RIFLE WAS HEAVY AT 11 LBS.

REAR SIGHT PROTECTOR

SIX ROUND MAGAZINE, PLUS ONE IN THE CHAMBER

SPRINGFIELD OR ENFIELD?

Was the Springfield the U.S. army's rifle of choice in WWI? Yes it was. However, nearly half the soldiers in WWI were issued American Enfield rifles. Factories couldn't produce enough Springfields, but factories that had built Enfields for the British were quiet. After some quick retooling, the American Enfield rifle was born. The Springfield was a fine rifle, and extremely accurate, the perfect rifle for America's doughboy marksmen. But so was the Enfield. Sergeant York was said to have used the American Enfield on his epic battle with the German army.

THE BIG SHOW

This was to be the Big Show. The final battle of WWI was the gigantic Meuse-Argonne Offensive, and for America it was the bloodiest ever, with 25,000 killed. This was also the end of trench warfare; combat was out in the open again, with a correspondingly high casualty rate. Without much combat experience, and depending on training manuals, the American forces were in for a rough time. Outdated trench warfare thinking still prevailed, such as how a barrage needed to be followed by a frontal attack. However, the Americans didn't lack courage, or tenacity, and commanders soon learned through experience. The Brown Automatic Rifle (BAR) was first used in the Battle of the Argonne Forest, and was much appreciated.

There is a mystery about why the army didn't issue the admittedly few BARs more promptly. It was said that army higher-ups, perhaps even General Pershing himself, thought of it as a secret weapon. If introduced too early in small numbers, they feared a BAR might be captured by Germans, copied by them, and used against U.S. troops.

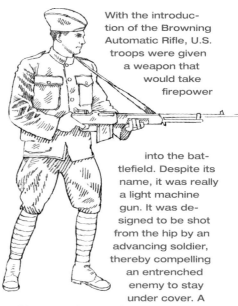

With the introduction of the Browning Automatic Rifle, U.S. troops were given a weapon that would take firepower into the battlefield. Despite its name, it was really a light machine gun. It was designed to be shot from the hip by an advancing soldier, thereby compelling an entrenched enemy to stay under cover. A problem was that it only carried twenty cartridges and was heavy for one-man operation.

THE HUN

PERHAPS DOUGHBOYS WEREN'T IN THE FIELD LONG ENOUGH TO SETTLE ON JUST ONE WORD TO DESCRIBE THEIR ADVERSARY. AMERICAN NEWSPAPERS FAVORED "HUN," BUT THE TYPICAL LETTER HOME USED MANY NAMES.

All armies need discipline, but the German army demanded total obedience. In the view of the Allies, German soldiers were expected to have no sentiment or self-pity and were brutal, fiercely patriotic, and impervious to fear. Even so, most new soldiers

These sturdy German army fellows, probably sergeants, sit with a sign that proclaims they are still thinking of home, though they are far away.

America is famously a nation of immigrants, and many immigrants were from Germany. These were solid people, hardworking, and thrifty, and they were loyal Americans. But Prime Minister Bismarck, then Kaiser Wilhelm, had established authoritarian rule back in Germany. In contrast, German immigrants in America flourished under its freedoms, and when called upon, they were loyal soldiers.

were just ordinary civilized young men. However, for those tutored by Prussian militarism, it was easy to play the stern martinet. And in this endless war, everyone fought savagely merely to survive.

A taste for severity and command are obvious in the stance of this young Prussian officer.

FRIGHTFULNESS

The doughboys crossing the ocean to save France and "Make the World Safe for Democracy" had heard of German "frightfulness," a word that implied both brutality and terrorist-like tactics. Examples of frightfulness included:

- The Rape of Belgium
- Unrestricted submarine warfare
- Poison gas
- International aggression to establish their "place in the sun"
- German kultur, which featured a cult of national superiority
- Prussian militarism

DUTCHMEN

For the doughboys, the soldiers of the German Empire were an enemy with many names. Some army higher-ups liked the word "boche," but it was usually pronounced to sound like "bushes," an unlikely name to describe a fierce enemy. "Prussians" might work because they were running the newly united Germany; however, Bavarian or Brandenburg regiments might be manning the trenches across no-man's-land. "Hun" was used by the press, rather than the troops. However, Hunland seemed like an excellent word for Germany. "Teutons" was once again a word that appealed mostly to the newsroom poets. The British liked "Fritz," as in "Old Fritz," and it was somewhat sympathetic. Many American letters home used the labels "Dutch" or "Dutchman," after Deutschland. In his letters Capt. Harry Truman used several terms, but favored Dutch.

Another choice word for Germans was "**Jerry**," the British slang word for chamber pot, which the German helmet resembled.

RAGTIME WAR

In the "teens" ragtime music was hugely popular in America. The Army took the music seriously and established the world's greatest ragtime band in France. At its head was Lt. James Europe, already a music legend, and an original black combat hero.

James Reese Europe was a human tornado, starting as a musical prodigy. While a young man, he became a bandleader, working with the famous dancers Vernon and Irene Castle, and his name became a household one. Always promoting the interests of African Americans, especially musicians, he was an activist and founded a society to protect their rights. When war came, he joined the army and was the first black officer to lead troops into battle in France. For his heroism he was awarded the Croix de Guerre. Eventually he was asked to form an army ragtime band, which soon delighted both American and French audiences. Still active in combat, and recovering from a gas attack, he composed "On Patrol in No Man's Land." This was a unique storytelling song, complete with battle sound effects. It became a nationwide hit.

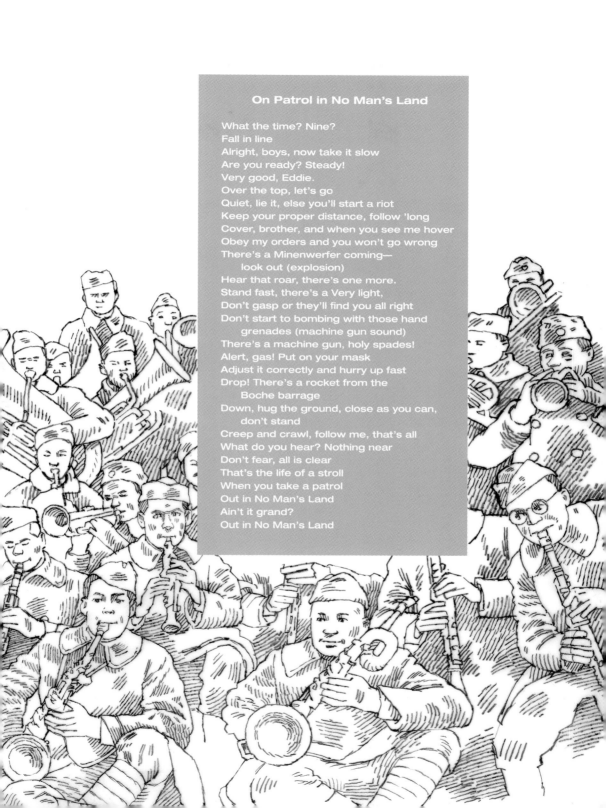

On Patrol in No Man's Land

What the time? Nine?
Fall in line
Alright, boys, now take it slow
Are you ready? Steady!
Very good, Eddie.
Over the top, let's go
Quiet, lie it, else you'll start a riot
Keep your proper distance, follow 'long
Cover, brother, and when you see me hover
Obey my orders and you won't go wrong
There's a Minenwerfer coming—
    look out (explosion)
Hear that roar, there's one more.
Stand fast, there's a Very light,
Don't gasp or they'll find you all right
Don't start to bombing with those hand
    grenades (machine gun sound)
There's a machine gun, holy spades!
Alert, gas! Put on your mask
Adjust it correctly and hurry up fast
Drop! There's a rocket from the
    Boche barrage
Down, hug the ground, close as you can,
    don't stand
Creep and crawl, follow me, that's all
What do you hear? Nothing near
Don't fear, all is clear
That's the life of a stroll
When you take a patrol
Out in No Man's Land
Ain't it grand?
Out in No Man's Land

LETTERS FROM HOME

MAIL WAS CENSORED TO DELETE ANYTHING OF MILITARY IMPORTANCE, WHICH MEANT THAT ANYTHING OF IMPORTANCE WAS REMOVED.

The army forbid both cameras and written journals, because they might fall into enemy hands. But some soldiers secretly recorded their experiences; others started journals and quit them. It was just too painful to remember. To paraphrase one ex-soldier when asked what combat was like; "They couldn't believe the things I've seen...crawling through mud filled with blood and excrement, and decomposed bodies of men and animals, with shells falling and German machine gun fire just over my head." So returning soldiers were quiet, and eventually people thought that Meuse-Argonne had been a cakewalk, which it was not.

THE BRIDGE OF SHIPS

The flotilla of troop and cargo ships that crossed the Atlantic was known as the **Bridge of Ships**. Letters from home were crucial to morale, and the nine-day crossing never seemed fast enough for the mail. As well were the intricacies at the French end of the line, which further slowed delivery. Some have estimated that as much as 50% of all mail went astray or was totally lost. Doughboys in Europe and the folks back home began putting consecutive numbers on each envelope, to keep track of the ones that didn't make it. The final destination would be to base camps behind the lines, though in some very quiet sectors, mail might be delivered to soldiers in the trenches.

SOMEWHERE IN FRANCE

Most American soldiers were young, and had never been away from home before. Getting a letter from home was almost like a visit from a loved one. It banished loneliness, and thoughts of war. However, writing home was not easy. Organizations such as the Red Cross or Knights of Columbus had established locations at base camps for relaxation and letter writing, and they provided paper and pencils. The army also had a short-form postcard where the doughboy could check off relevant options, such as "I am well" or "I am in the hospital and will contact you soon." Army secrecy required the letter writer to omit any reference to his location or activity. The opaque term **Somewhere in France** was the only address soldiers could give. Letters were reviewed by censors, and any sensitive information was blacked out by a thick pen. Letters with too many problems were returned to the sender, possibly with a reprimand. Army rules stated that "letter writing is a privilege not a right, and it could be revoked."

THE BLUES

Of course soldiers didn't want to worry folks back home, or offend the censors, so many doughboy letters had an oddly cheery feel. No matter how dire the situation, a few carefully selected euphemisms could paint a more acceptable picture.

- "Nothing much happening here, but the other day we saw a few shells. But those Huns sure have bad aim."

- "I'm happy about all the exercise I've been getting. And the French countryside sure is beautiful."

- "I enjoy the outdoor life. Next stop Berlin, then we'll kick Kaiser Bill in the pants."

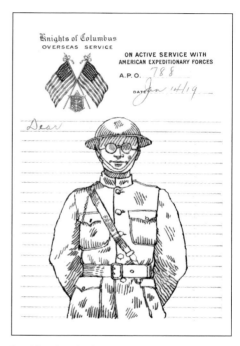

Looking back, Capt. Harry S. Truman has to be the most remembered WWI letter writer, with his daily "Dear Bess" letters to his Missouri sweetheart, and future first lady of the United States. The letters are filled with tender words for Bess, and pride in the part he played in the Meuse-Argonne Offensive. In October 1918 he wrote, "The papers are in the street now saying that the Central Powers have asked for peace, and I was in the drive that did it! I shot out a German battery, shot up his big observation post, and ruined another battery when it was moving down the road."

GROUNDHOG DAY

IN 1918 IN THE ELEVENTH MONTH, ON THE ELEVENTH DAY, AT ELEVEN IN THE MORNING, UNEXPECTEDLY FOR MANY, THE ARMISTICE WAS ANNOUNCED, AND FIGHTING ABRUPTLY STOPPED. THE JOKE AT THAT MOMENT WAS THAT THIS WAS GROUNDHOG DAY, WHEN TROOPS FINALLY EMERGED FROM THEIR UNDERGROUND BORROWS, AND ONCE AGAIN SAW THE SUN.

The awful German Spring Offensive had at last been stopped, and the Allies somehow remained standing. But in the fall of 1918, no one really believed the fighting would end soon. Allied preparations continued for their 1919 knock-out blow offensive. Vast armadas of aircraft capable of bombing deep in Germany were gathered. There would

be huge formations of tanks, and the A.E.F. would number four million men. However, the German army had been so ground down in the autumn of 1918 that continued resistance would be useless. It's said when the Armistice came, German soldiers often cheered louder than the Americans.

After all, the doughboys had just arrived and were still ready to go. Legend has it that Captain Harry Truman's unit reluctantly fired the last artillery shots of the war. Still there was great jubilation on that day. The Armistice was the one event that was universally recorded in letters and memoirs. Often the words were inclined to the ecstatic and poetic.

"PEACE! I'm writing this at 11:30, the morning of November 11th—the greatest day in history. The armistice has just been signed and the last shot was fired at 11:00. Talk about noise—the men, yelling, cheering, the remaining church bells clanging, every available rifle and machinegun firing. The old refugees crying—oh what a grand an' glorious feeling."

—Ralph S. Gordon

"The gun fire quit, the sun came out, the wind stopped blowing, and the church bells in Andilly started ringing. A feeling of contentment came over us. We felt like our job in France was done and we would soon be going home."

—Roy C. Harper

Drawings left and right represent two memorial statues in New York City.

Normalcy Returns

THE WORLD WAR WAS AN EVENT OF UNIMAGINABLE SCOPE. AND IN MANY WAYS IT DIDN'T REALLY END. CIVIL WAR CONTINUED IN RUSSIA UNTIL 1922, IN 1920 POLAND DEFEATED THE BOLSHEVIKS IN THE BATTLE OF WARSAW, IN 1922 THE FASCIST LEADER MUSSOLINI TOOK POWER IN ITALY—AND SO ON.

A MIST FROM THE SOUL

Victorian authors might have called it ectoplasm; some called it "soul mist." It is the elusive glowing purple fog that is reported to exit the body of a dying person. It was seen, if we are to believe the stories, streaming upward from the bodies of countless British soldiers who, rank upon rank, were mowed down in no-man's-land.

There is a poetic truth to these stories, but psychologists can explain away things like this, such as the misty fog that seems to cross the room soon after the death of a loved one. It has something to do with grieving, confusion, and emotional overload. And just consider the death of more than five million Allied soldiers on the Western Front. The number was beyond all sense or reason. The grief was overwhelming, yet for the survivors, one way or another, life went on.

Most survivors, military or civilian, bore their pain privately and silently. And then there were those grieving souls who turned to spiritualists in an attempt to contact sons, husbands, and brothers who had never come back. It was a sad quest, since it was frauds and charlatans who offered false comfort.

Publicly, nations, cities, and towns created memorials. By one estimate in the United States alone there were ten thousand WWI memorials erected, including two thousand statues.

Another way to honor the war dead was political, especially an attempt to create a community of nations. The hope was to create an international order where peace would be a permanent reality. The first and best advocate for this peace-loving League of Nations was President Woodrow Wilson. But after America's brief and painful excursion in world affairs, heartland politicians wanted no more foreign entanglements. Wilson suffered a massive stroke, and his wife secretly assumed the role of political caretaker; but because of American opposition, the League suffered a near-fatal blow even before it was officially born.

The year 1919 was one of the worst supposedly "peace-time" years in history. American soldiers were still in Russia and Siberia fighting the Bolsheviks. Back home we had the Boston Police Strike, the Seattle General Strike, and the Red Scare, plus the anti-leftist Palmer Raids, which arrested ten thousand people. In 1920 candidate Warren Harding called for a return to pre-WWI values, or as his campaign put it, "a return to normalcy."

WAR—AS WE KNOW IT

Published in the June 13, 1919, issue of *Stars and Stripes* last editorial was the following:

"This summer is the last the A.E.F., as most of us know it, will sweat through (in the German occupation). We've finished and we have the satisfaction of knowing that we did a good job and we're glad to quit.

But can we carry the lesson home? Print can't do it.

Photographs can't do it.

Many will come to Belleau Wood, people who have read all about the Great War.

Already worn paths scar that once pathless hell. Those people will see the twisted trees. But they won't see the sprawling forms beneath them. They will see the bullet-bitten rocks. But they can never visualize the trembling horror of lying in those crevices while the German guns spat their death through the grass. Here and there they may pick up an empty shell. But the fingerless hands protruding from the rotting khaki blouse has been graciously buried beneath a neat white cross.

The horror has been hallowed. The misery has become picturesque, the murder turned to romance.

And those little villages in the valleys! Their strange, sad windows look out across fresh meadows now like staring blinded eyes. They are so still, so deathly still—not a single wisp of friendly smoke, no human color, only a garish patch perhaps where some unremembered bush flaunts its green branch across the gray.

This cannot touch the tourist. The home folks can never feel it beside their friendly hearths. Nobody under God's great tranquil skies can tell the rottenness of war but the men who suffered through it.

Upon them rests a solemn duty. They must go home and choke the coward jingo who masks himself behind his false and blatant patriotism and the merchant-politician not content with stuffing his coffers till they burst—but anxious to barter the blood of his country's young manhood for a new place in the sun.

The Prussian Guardsman died hard, fighting for such a place. The men in frock coats who make the laws never had to stand up against him. They never took a machine gun nest, or ever saw a barrage roll down, then uncurtain a wall of shrieking steel. We know what the Prussian Guardsman means—his code, his cold courage, and blind patriotism that sent him forward, granting none the right to live but those who wore his uniform.

We know, but we cannot give that knowledge to others. But upon it we can act. We can help build a League of Nations with such sinews of war, and such conscience for peace that no one will dare oppose it.

If we don't, the blood will be on our foolish heads, which by the grace of God, chance, or some Prussian Guardsman's poor aim, are still on our foolish shoulders."

Believing in such views or not, the doughboys came marching home, and everyone cheered, then went back to business as usual.

And thank goodness for that, because it was still so much worse in Europe.

Bibliography

Barbusse, Henri. *Under Fire*. New York: Penguin Books, 2003.

Barker, Pat. *Regeneration*. New York: Plume, 1993.

Barthas, Louis. *The World War I Notebooks of Corporal Louis Barthas, Barrelmaker, 1914-1918*. New Haven: Yale University Press, 2015.

Blom, Philipp. *The Vertigo Years: Europe, 1900-1914*. New York: Basic Books, 2008.

Emmerson, Charles. *1913: In Search of the World before the Great War*. New York: Public Affairs, 2013.

Empey, Arthur Guy. *First Call*. New York: G.P. Putnam, 1918.

Empey, Arthur Guy. *Over the Top*. New York: G.P. Putnam, 1918.

Englund, Peter. *The Beauty and the Sorrow*. New York: Alfred A. Knopf, 2011.

Falls, Cyril. *The Great War*. New York: G.P. Putnam, 1959.

Fussell, Paul. *The Great War and Modern Memory*. New York: Oxford University Press, 1975.

Gilbert, Martin. *The First World War*. New York: Henry Holt, 1994.

Graves, Robert. *Good-Bye to All That*. New York: Penguin Books, 2000.

Hagedorn, Ann. *Savage Peace: Hope and Fear in America, 1919*. New York: Simon & Schuster, 2007.

Hart, Peter. *The Great War*. New York: Oxford University Press, 2013.

Horne, Alistair. *The Price of Glory: Verdun 1916*. New York: Penguin Books, 1993.

Jones, Barbara, and Howell, Bill. *Popular Arts of the First World War*. New York: McGraw-Hill, 1972.

Keegan, John. *The First World War*. New York: Alfred A. Knopf, 1999.

Laskin, David. *The Long Way Home: An American Journey from Ellis Island to the Great War*. New York: Harper Perennial, 2011.

Macdonald, Lyn. *To the Last Man*. New York: Carroll and Graf Publishers, 1999.

MacMillan, Margaret. *Paris 1919: Six Months That Changed the World*. New York: Random House, 2003.

Middlebrook, Martin. *The First Day on the Somme, 1 July 1916*. New York: W.W. Norton, 1972.

Nagel, Fritz. *Fritz: The World War I Memoir of a German Lieutenant*. Huntington, W.Va: Blue Acorn Press, 1981.

Paschall, Rod. *The Defeat of Imperial Germany, 1917-1918*. Chapel Hill: Algonquin Books of Chapel Hill, 1989.

Reynolds, David. *The Long Shadow: The Legacies of the Great War in the Twentieth Century*. New York: W.W. Norton, 2013.

Rolt-Wheeler, Francis. *The Wonder of War on Land*. Boston: Lothrop, Lee & Shepard, 1918.

Russell, Thomas H. *America's War for Humanity: Pictorial History of the World War for Liberty*. Toledo, Ohio; Homewood Press, 1919.

Sassoon, Siegfried. *Memoirs of a Fox-Hunting Man*. New York: Penguin Books, 2013.

Sassoon, Siegfried. *Memoirs of an Infantry Officer*. New York: Penguin Books, 2013.

Smith, Leonard V. *Between Mutiny and Obedience: The Case of the French Fifth Infantry Division during World War 1*. Princeton: Princeton University Press, 1994.

Tuchman, Barbara. *The Proud Tower*. New York: Macmillan, 1966.

Vansittart, Peter. *Voices from the Great War*. New York: Franklin Watts, 1984.

White, B.T. *Tanks and Other Armored Fighting Vehicles, 1900-1918*. New York: Macmillan, 1970.

Glossary

l'abri: bunker, dugout

l'aero: airplane

aileron: wing flap of an airplane

une auge: literally "a trough," but meaning a soldier's plate

les bandes molletières: leggings

la becquetance: soldier's grub

le bidasse: messmate

le bidon: canteen

le biffin: looking like a rag picker

le boche: French slang for a German

la Bochie: French slang for Germany

la bouillasse: muck, mud

un boyau: communication trench (literally, intestine or gut); the entrance to a trench

la cafard: the depression; literally, "the cockroach"

canard: literally "duck"; slang for sniper, as they would pop up, take a quick shot, and then go down again

la capote: greatcoat or overcoat

la casque: helmet

un cerf: literally "a deer"; a skilled cavalryman and his horse

ceux: literally "them"; used derisively to refer to the lucky, or pampered, rear troops who were not ordered to the front lines

Char Renault tank: a small French tank that would mean the end of trench warfare

Chauchat: a light portable machine gun designed by Colonel Chauchat

une cisaille: shears

la cloche: literally "the bell"; the helmet designed by Adrian made of thin steel; later inspired ladies' hats

la commotion: shell shock

le coupe de main: raid, raid in force

le créneau: loophole or observation slit in trench for snipers

le danse: the fight

le fanfaron: scoundrel

fantassin: a French infantry soldier; the notion of infant or child is associated with both the French and English word

le flingue: the rifle, or gun

fuselage: body of an airplane

la gamelle individuelle: mess kit; literally, "individual bowl"

le gaz: gas

le got: the flea

le groin de cochon: a gas mask; literally, "pig snout," referring to the shape of the mask

un gros noir: a type of artillery shell, named after its heavy black smoke

une hache: ax

Hotchkiss: the primary French machine gun in WWI

kepi: the round, straight-sided cap with the leather peak worn by gendarmes

le lapin: literally "the rabbit"; the clever, brave French soldier (*see also* System D)

livret individuel: paybook

le machine à découdre: the un-sewing machine; the machine gun that could rip anything, or anyone, to pieces

le marmite: a big stewpot

un moineau: type of artillery shell; literally, a sparrow, because of the sound it made when flying over the soldiers

le moulin à café: machine gun; literally, coffee grinder

nacelle: housing for crew or engine within an airplane

Old Charles: Georges Guynemer's nickname for his personal SPAD plane

P.C.D.F: "poor victims at the front," approximately translated; nickname the exhausted poilus in the trenches gave themselves

la pantalon-culottes: culotte trousers

une pelle bêche: shovel spade

un pernod: a type of artillery shell, named after its green smoke (like the drink Pernod)

péteux: a bad soldier; one who is careless or lazy (literally, "pheasant")

petite blessé: the walking wounded

pinard: wine drunk by French soldiers

le poilu: literally "one who is hairy"; a French soldier

les pompes: soldier's boots; the "pump" is an old name for certain shoes; going up and down like a pump-piston might be the word origin

le puce: all insect pests

le quart: a small military cup

rollers: wheeled field kitchens (French: *roulantes*)

les roulantes: *see* rollers

le sac à terre: sandbag

schrapnells: undercooked peas or beans

une scie: saw

le séchoir: barbed wire or clothesline; the term referred to soldiers killed and fallen onto the wire, as if hung out to dry

le singe: monkey meat

la soupe: in the mornings, and in the afternoons, meals were usually a stew, and they were always called this

SPAD: French biplane

stabilisateur: elevator or horizontal stabilizer of an airplane

System D: a resourceful, scrappy way of life French soldiers followed to improvise

le tire-boche: the bayonet; literally "the boche-screw" (*see* boche)

le toto: the louse

le village détruit: villages that had been destroyed in the line of fire, possibly with unexploded munitions left behind; literally "destroyed villages"

zimboum: a type of artillery shell, named for the sound it made

zinzin: a type of artillery shell, named for the sound it made

alleyman: the German enemy

axle grease: butter

barker: see barking iron

barking iron: Webley revolver, taking its name from nineteenth-century dueling pistols (*see also* barker)

battle bowler: see Brodie helmet

battle police: armed military police deployed in trenches during an attack to discourage stragglers

Belgian rattlesnake: Lewis light machine gun

belly flop: falling to the ground quickly during an enemy attack, or when hit

bivvy: a temporary shelter, bivouac

Black HandGang: an ironic name for British trench raiders

Blighty: slang for home, for British soldiers (*see also* Blighty One); from the Hindi for "home"

Blighty One: a serious but not fatal wound; the type of wound that would send a British soldier back home to "Dear Old Blighty," as opposed to one that would kill, maim, or debilitate him

body snatcher: a Tommy on a night raid; or a sniper; or a stretcher bearer

Brodie helmet: named after inventor John Brodie's 1915 design, a shallow hat with a wide brim made of tough manganese steel

bully beef: corned beef

char: "tea" in Hindi

chit: a note or receipt, from Hindi

clicked it: to be killed

come-along: a length of barbed wire with a loop that was slipped over a captured enemy's neck and pulled like a leash

coot: the ever-present louse

crummy: itchy from insect bites

cubbyhole: see funk hole

cushy: easy or pleasant, such as a "cushy job"; from Hindi

dekko: a look or glance around in order to observe, from Hindi

dixie: a large backpack-like container

duckboard: wooden walkway on trench floor

dud: an unexploded shell; during the Battle of the Somme, dud shell rates were as high as 30%

elephant dugout: large dugout

Emma Gee: machine gun, playing off of military phonetics (MG)

fed-up: originally from the Boer War

fee: Vickers F.E.8, an early fighter plane

five rounds rapid: an order given to still-groggy British troops each morning to fire quick rifle shots at the German line, in an effort to maintain a martial spirit (*see also* mad minute and morning hate)

for it: in trouble

funk hole: one-man shelter scraped out of the side of a trench

gasper: a cheap cigarette

gippo: currant pudding

grab a packet: to be hit by enemy fire

grubber: an entrenching tool; a small shovel to dig a new trench

gun bus: Vickers F.B.5, an early fighter plane

hot cross bun: an ambulance, which prominently displayed the Red Cross symbol

in front: to be in no-man's-land

the Jack Johnson: a German howitzer shell 8 to 9 inches in caliber, and on impact it sent up columns of greasy black smoke

jankers: minor punishment

khaki: light yellow camouflage color, or uniform of that color; standard uniform of that color begun to be used by the British army at the turn of the twentieth century; linguistic origins from Persian and Urdu, meaning "dusty"

kultur: so-called superior German civilization, especially its rigid and brutal military aspect; grimly humorous

lance jack: lance corporal, a British rank just below corporal

landowner: someone who is dead and buried

Mad Jack: nickname for Siegfried Sassoon, British officer who excelled at night raids

mad minute: see five rounds rapid

moaning Minnie: referred to the German trench mortar or Minenwerfer, the term carrying overtones of familiarity and humor

mob: the unit, company, or battalion

morning hate: see five rounds rapid

mud: the all-pervasive environmental feature of northern France and Belgium

mufti: civilian dress, from the Arabic meaning "free"

near go: familiar nineteenth-century British slang for "a close call"

night roll: an ambulance out on a nighttime mission

nix: "no," from the German "nicht"

the nonstop: an enemy shell that has passed well overhead

on the peg: to be put on charge

on the wire: killed, as in the song "Hanging on the Old Barbed Wire"

parapet: the trench top that Tommy had to climb over

persuader: a heavy wooden club with protruding nails; for use during silent night raids on enemy trenches

pig-nose: British Small Box Respirator gas mask with a round snout

pozzy: jam

putt: see puttee

puttee: leg wraps worn instead of boots (see also putt)

redcaps: military police

rest camp: a cemetery

ricco: a ricocheted bullet

rolling barrage: a slowly moving curtain of artillery fire that just barely preceded the troops as they crossed no-man's-land

rum: distributed every morning; especially welcome while waiting for zero hour

S.R.D.: initials of Service Ration Depot printed on tots of rum distributed to soldiers; jokingly renamed "Soon Runs Dry" or "Seldom Reaches Destination" by Tommies

sandbag street: the firing line (see also shooting gallery)

sapping: a safer, more roundabout method of digging trenches, by starting at either end and working inward

shackles: soup or stew made from leftovers

shooting gallery: the firing line, or front line

the silent Susan: a high-velocity shell

smelly: Lee Enfield rifle; its official nickname was "Short, Magazine, Lee-Enfield" or SMLE Mk III

snuffed it: to be killed, as a candle is snuffed

spotted dog: meat pudding

stiff's paddock: burial ground

strafe: the German word for "to punish," or "to worry or confound"; eventually, it meant to rake with gunfire, especially from an airplane

suicide squad: the men who operated machine guns, called thus because of their short life expectancy

teakettle: a steam locomotive, especially a narrow gauge one

thrown a seven: killed; bad luck, mate

tin hat: see Brodie helmet

trench cats: cats in substantial numbers went to war, as mousers and mascots; they were also used to locate poison gas, in what must have been a suicide mission

trench frogs: on occasion a plague of croaking frogs would descend on the waterlogged trenches; walking in trenches filled with squirming creatures was unnerving

trench journals: because official news was censored, many British outfits published their own newspapers; much of the content was humorous or irreverent, and the most famous was "The Wipers Times," named after Ypres (the place and the battle)

trench mouth: one of many diseases brought on by stress and deprivation; bleeding gums and foul breath were symptoms

Uncle Charlie: the order to march with full equipment, a burden weighing in at 66 lbs. or so

wash basin: *see* Brodie helmet

wave: one of several lines of men who go over the top in an attack

windy: to be nervous or apprehensive, as in before an attack

woodbine: brand of cheap cigarettes

American

black jack coffee: coffee made by adding cold water to strong coffee before it boils over

blotto: totally drunk, to the point of unconsciousness

bozo: a stupid, inept, rude person, or clown; probably an early vaudeville character

Bridge of Ships: the flotilla of troop and cargo ships that crossed the Atlantic

buddy: a comrade or valued friend; it was thought by some soldiers that this term came from New York City, where they assumed everyone was called "buddy"

busted: demoted

cherched: getting some needed piece of equipment, or any other thing. It is comparable to scrounge, or some would call it, borrowing while neglecting to obtain permission

conked out: refers to an airplane engine stopping mid-flight; the word is said to reproduce the last sounds of the failing engine, conk-conk-conk

devil dogs: German nickname for U.S. Marines

dogs: feet

doughboy: an American soldier; the origin of the term is still debated, but it seems to go back to the 1848 Mexican War, when the uniforms of marching American soldiers were white with flour-like Mexican dust

doughgirl: the female version of doughboy, but applied to the young women of the Red Cross, who were well known for passing out doughnuts

dry rub: when water is not available, a method of vigorously dry rubbing with a coarse towel as a substitute for bathing

frog: a derisive name for the French

gadget: a catch-all term for any newfangled contraption or thing, but mostly referring to a mechanical device, usually of a puzzling nature

goldfish: canned salmon

gone west: a euphemism for "died"

Great War: how World War I was known to the doughboys in the trenches at the time, as well as most other people

hardboiled: a quality a doughboy takes on after losing the soft, squishy insides of a civilian, now believing instead that conventional morality counts for nothing

hop-over: a short duration raid into enemy territory

jake: meaning everything is fine, or cool; first used in 1914, it may have been a corruption of the French word "chic"

kaput: from the German, meaning finished or done

knock koo-koo: to knock out, knock unconscious, or kill

land battleship: an early name for British army tanks

lid: a steel helmet

looking their best: coats shortened to solve the problem of long overcoats weighed down by mud; hair trimmed short to discourage lice

muleskinners: foul-mouthed handlers of mules for trekking the terrain of muddy northern France

nobon: no good

outfit: a cowboy word borrowed for war use; any group of men, from a platoon to an army, might qualify

pass: to die

Prohibition: the constitutional amendment of 1919 to ban the sale of alcohol; this also affected the U.S. army

pull-through: a piece of cloth used to clean rifles

punk: bread, as it was called in prewar New York City breadlines

pushing up daisies: to be killed and buried in France

replacements: those who came to replace fallen men in an outfit that had trained together

roughneck: artilleryman

shellitis: experiencing the horror of war firsthand; an initial first step toward eventual shell shock

somewhere in France: the opaque term soldiers were allowed to use as their only address in letters home, to pass the censors

through the mill: state of an army unit that had persevered through the front lines; originally referred to working in a hot and dangerous steel mill

wig-wag: the flag waving cross-field signal system first used in the Civil War

Y.M.: short for Y.M.C.A.

INDEX

Acknowledgments

I want to thank the many people who assisted and encouraged me during this book's long period of gestation. Foremost would be my wife, who once again encouraged me to follow my bliss. Then there is my longtime publisher and friend, Marta Hallett, who recognized that my unusual project might someday be a viable book.

Thanks also to the following friends and colleagues for their assistance: Frank Sullivan, my co-author on previous publishing projects. He has always been a dependable sounding board for my endless musings. Sarah Newell, her gracious hospitality, and love of London's history made our 2014 visit there a delight. Jane Knight, unsurpassed hostess, travel guide, and dear friend who whisked us through the winding lanes of county Kent to new WWI-themed adventures every day. Jane also provided information about her grandfather, Charlie Adolphus Sampson, who had been a British Medical Officer for the duration of the war. His story is told in the British chapter. Thanks also to the superb illustrator George Gaadt, who introduced me to the world of WWI reenactors. And thanks to the reenacters I met and photographed in Pennsylvania; their dedication to keeping history alive is a wonder.

Also thanks to the great Ed Vebel: collector, artist, and a real-life WWII American in Paris; and Rick Keller who offered his incredible personal collection of WWI artifacts. The Great War Association, an international organization with local chapters around the world, offers a website that is an excellent introduction to a full range of WWI boots-on-the-ground information. Also helpful was the National World War I Museum in Kansas City, Missouri, which gave me permission to use several outstanding vintage photographs as reference. Project Gutenberg, that vast online library of copyright-free books, is a wonderful source of early twentieth century information.

Mention also must be made of the following institutions: The picture collection of the New York Public Library, with its extensive files of World War I photographs. And in the UK, The Imperial War Museum, Duxford, the aviation site of the Imperial War Museum; Chatham Historic Dockyard; Dover Castle's WWI artillery control bunker; and the London Transport Museum, each of which provided invaluable resource in compiling information and art.

Especially memorable in 2014 were the nearly one million red ceramic poppies circling the Tower of London, one for each British and Commonwealth soldier lost in World War I. Much of the reference for this book came from my own collection and photographs.